C000178259

BEYOND THE _ _ _

A Collection of Poems & Writings
Celebrating the Centenary of
George Mackay Brown (1921–1996)

Edited by
Jim Mackintosh & Paul S Philippou

Foreword by
Asif Khan, Director of the Scottish Poetry Library

TIPPERMUIR
· BOOKS LIMITED ·

Beyond the Swelkie – Jim Mackintosh & Paul S Philippou (Editors).
Copyright © 2021. All rights reserved.

The right of the contributors to the book (as listed therein) to be
identified as the authors of the Work has been asserted in accordance
with the Copyright, Designs & Patents Act 1988.

This first edition published and copyright 2021 by
Tippermuir Books Ltd, Perth, Scotland.
mail@tippermuirbooks.co.uk — www.tippermuirbooks.co.uk.

ISBN 978-1-913836-08-5 (paperback).
A CIP catalogue record for this book is available from the British Library.

Project coordination by Dr Paul S Philippou.
Cover design by Matthew Mackie.
Editorial support: Ajay Close and Steve Zajda.
Text design, layout, and artwork by Bernard Chandler [graffik].
Text set in Din Regular 9.5/15pt with Din Bold titling.

Printed and bound by CPI Group (UK) Ltd, Croydon CR0 4YY.

ACKNOWLEDGEMENTS

The editors wish to acknowledge the many people, who in different ways contributed to this book. Foremostly, we would like to acknowledge those who responded to our appeal for poems and prose and entrusted us with their wonderful creations. When we started out, we were unaware how good the body of work that *Beyond the Swelkie* would eventually comprise. We acknowledge that for others the constraints of time and other demands left them unable to contribute – they are here in spirit. Asif Khan requires special thanks for his foreword which really sets the scene for the pages which follow and anchors the book to the Scottish Poetry Library and poetry in Scotland and beyond.

During the early stages of the book, we reached out to the George Mackay Brown Fellowship and others working on the centenary of George Mackay Brown's birth. We thank these groups and organisations for their friendliness and welcome.

Many others gave their time and effort to see to the realisation of this project. Steve Zajda, as ever Tippermuir's faithful and vigilant proof-reader. Unlike with chess where a computer did eventually beat a human, software will never replace those eagle-eyed or pedantic proof-readers – they are the gods among us.

The following individuals deserve special praise:

George Gunn for offering us an initial sense of connection to George Mackay Brown, for steering us in the right direction as the project was birthed and for helping us to go above and 'beyond the swelkie'.

Alexander (Sandy) Moffat for allowing us to use his portrait of George Mackay Brown for the cover and to adapt its form to suit the book.

Andy Jackson who gave impetus and assistance to the book in its early stages.

Stuart A Paterson and Gerry Cambridge for sourcing the drawing of George Mackay Brown by Alasdair Gray which was previously published in *Spectrum* magazine in 1996.

Matthew Mackie for his cover that even before the publication of the book received veneration.

Bernard Chandler for his skills in the arts of graphics that has helped produce a beautiful looking book.

To all others involved in this book, we offer our sincere thanks and appreciation.

Some of the poems in the book have appeared either in full, in part or in form elsewhere:

'Weaving the Threads' (Pamela Beasant) was first published in *Slightly Foxed* magazine in 2016.

'The Ocean of Time' (Stewart Conn) is from *Stolen Light: Selected Poems* (1999) and appears with permission from the publisher, Bloodaxe Books.

'Nae Rhyme or Reason' (Jo Gilbert) was a commission by StAnza International Poetry Festival in 2021.

An earlier version of 'Caithness' (John Glenday) appeared in the *Café Review*.

A version of 'Leaving Harbour' (Andrew Greig) was first published as 'Post script' in memory of George Mackay Brown in *Found at Sea* (2013).

'Fear a' Bhàta – Cèilidh Buan'/'The Boatman – Everlasting Cèilidh' (Màiri Anna NicUalraig/Mary Ann Kennedy) is from *Talamh Beò* (Living Land), a music and poetry commission for the Coigach & Assynt Living Landscape Partnership.

'Leaving the Island' (Stuart A Paterson) was first published in *Saving Graces* in 1997.

'Warbeth Walk' (Nalini Paul) was first published on the StAnza International Poetry Festival website in 2015 as part of their 'Poetry Map of Scotland' project. The poem was recorded by sound artist Suzy Angus and broadcast in April 2015 on the pop-up radio station, Radiophrenia.

'The Lit Room' (Sheenagh Pugh) was first published in *The Beautiful Lie* (2002) and later in *Later Selected Poems* (2009).

EDITORS' NOTE

In the first paragraph of *An Orkney Tapestry*, George Mackay Brown described the swirl and boil of the Pentland Firth and the maelstrom, known locally as the 'Swelkie', which makes any journey across it an adventure in both directions. It was this challenge that inspired the naming of the book as *Beyond The Swelkie*, a title that reflects George Mackay Brown's reach outwards from Orkney to draw people into his world and his looking inwards for inspiration – a cultural gravitational pull that worked in two directions and one which acted upon and influenced this book. Given the extraordinary times we have all recently endured, there is an added relevance to the phrase as we look beyond the maelstrom of the pandemic and the uncertainty it has created, in particular in the creative arts.

After some consideration, it was determined that the book would offer a blank canvas to poets, writers, friends and family of Brown and academics to make a contribution to the centenary, be it poetry, short prose or essay. The result is a truly marvellous smörgåsbord of writing that celebrates and acknowledges Brown's contribution to twentieth-century poetry and literature, as well as entertains and informs.

In making the choice as to who to ask to contribute to the book, the editors were acutely aware of the need for a balance and breadth of styles, approaches and experiences, as well as cultural diversity. It is hoped that *Beyond the Swelkie* has achieved that balance. Thanks and praise go to all the contributors to the book – it is a testament to them all that the process of editing ran remarkably smoothly. That said, any errors in the book are those of the editors alone.

Offering a blank canvas was somewhat of a scary proposition for the editors. What was received from the contributors demonstrated that poetry and literary studies have survived the pandemic, healthier and heartier than before.

There are common themes among the contributions, the importance to many of Brown's poem 'Beachcomber' being modal. And, there are several contributions that are unique individual responses to Brown. Taken as a whole, the book can only be that tip of the celebratory iceberg which Brown's corpus and life warrants. *Beyond the Swelkie* is one small node in a network of publications, events and interactions with Brown in his centenary year. It is hoped that this book will assist that network to do justice to Brown's legacy.

As this 'Editors' Note' is being written, the pandemic in Scotland is evolving and it may be that soon literary events will once again be live 'physical' happenings. The poetry, prose and essays in *Beyond the Swelkie* deserve to be read by a wide audience, but moreover, they need to be performed, read aloud and discussed.

In selecting an order for the poems, short prose and essays which comprise *Beyond the Swelkie*, the editors were minded that the 'blank canvas' approach mitigated against an overall structured narrative. Consequently, there are two main sections to the book. The first is made up of poems and short prose while the second is made up of essays – longer pieces of prose. In both sections, contributions appear in an alphabetical order according to the surname of the contributor. It was felt, nonetheless, that these sections required 'bookends' to create a unified book, and to this end, a preface and postscript have been created, drawn from two of the contributions – those by Fiona MacInnes and Andrew Greig, respectively.

All that remains is to send the reader into the pages that follow and, following Brown, to do so, by first *spilling water of blessing over the threshold*. Enjoy!

Jim Mackintosh and Paul S Philippou
June 2021

CONTENTS

ESSAYS

POSTSCRIPT

FOREWORD

Asif Khan

When I took over the helm of the Scottish Poetry Library in June 2016, the library was offered the long-term loan of a portrait of George Mackay Brown painted by Ian MacInnes, a life-long friend of the Orkney poet, and former art teacher at Stromness Academy. MacInnes had illustrated many of George's books as well as painting several portraits of him. The painting being offered was the same portrait that was used on the original edition of Mackay Brown's memoir, *For the Islands I Sing*.

The title of the autobiography reprises the first line of Mackay Brown's debut collection, *The Storm*, which was published by Orkney Press in 1955. Kathleen Jamie in her introduction to the second edition of the book wrote that the debut announced Mackay Brown as, '…uncommonly sure of his place and his concerns', adding, '…these are not the unsteady beginnings of a young poet finding his place or fretting about his right to speak. Here already is the Orcadian local-as-universal'.[1] To my mind, the MacInnes portrait perfectly captured the confident *arriviste* of whom Jamie asserted was on a path to become 'one of the greatest Scottish writers of his age'.[2]

Chapman magazine commissioned George Mackay Brown along with Norman MacCaig, Ian Crichton Smith and Sorley Maclean to express what motivated and sustained their poetry.

1 George Mackay Brown, *The Storm and Other Poems* (2017), p.9.

2 Brown, *The Storm and Other Poems*, p.11.

Mackay Brown reflected that Christ's parable of a man's life akin to a seed cast into a furrow, '...illuminated the whole of life for me, it made everything simple and marvellous. It included within itself everything, from the most primitive of the breaking of the soil to Christ himself with his parables of the agriculture and the majestic symbolism of his passion, and death and resurrection'.[3]

Mackay Brown continued that a poem titled 'Stations of the Cross', in which Christ's passion is counterpointed by the work of the crofter, was a key poem for anyone who is interested in his writing. Commonly, the Stations of the Cross is presented as a visual or literal depiction of a series of 14 images of Christ's path from condemnation to crucifixion to entombment. Pilgrims will commonly stop at each station to say selected prayers and reflections. As an example, Mackay Brown wrote of Christ's third fall under the weight of the cross:

> Third Fall
> Scythes are sharpened to bring you down,
> King Barleycorn.

The Stations of the Cross is also a motif to be found in Mackay Brown's prose writing, with the sea replacing the soil as the setting for legendary Viking Earl Rognvald and his fellow crusaders following Christ's journey as 'a young hero-skipper guiding his ship into the rage of history'.[4]

In a review of Maggie Fergusson's biography of Mackay Brown, Dennis O'Driscoll wrote that Brown's poems were often structured around rudimentary cycles: the seasons, the days

---

3 *Chapman*, 16 (1976), p.23.

4 George Mackay Brown, *For the Islands I Sing* (1997), p.170.

of the week, the months of the year or the Stations of the Cross. 'Sometimes, his words filled these forms mechanically, like ready-made moulds; at their brilliant best, though, the poems are flooded with the light of revelation and illumination like the Neolithic tomb at Maes Howe....'[5]

Mackay Brown believed that all of life's experiences and journeys were 'drenched with symbol'.[6] Alan Bold, in his critical study of Mackay Brown, thought that the poet was something of a law unto himself: a man activated by a wide artistic vision. Mackay Brown did not deal with unseemly city life but revealed a great island landscape whose work was informed with legend and myth and image and symbol. 'He is very much his own man', wrote Bold.[7]

Mackay Brown rarely ventured far from his home in Stromness, Orkney. He had spent some time in Edinburgh, firstly at Newton Abbey College from 1951 to 1952 under the tutelage of fellow Orcadian poet Edwin Muir, and then as a student at the University of Edinburgh from 1956 to 1960, from where he graduated with an MA in English. At this time, Mackay Brown would have become versed in the Old Norse sagas in translation. The *Orkneyinga Saga* and story of St Magnus the Orkney warrior-martyr fuelled Mackay Brown's interest throughout his career. N D Garriock suggested that the narrative technique of the sagas 'permeates' Mackay Brown's work.[8]

Mackay Brown's social life often involved the writers and artists who gathered in the Rose Street pubs of Milne's Bar

---

5 'The poet who lived the shy life', *The Irish Times*, 20 May 2006.

6 *Chapman*, 60 (1990), p.3.

7 Alan Bold, *George Mackay Brown: Modern Writer Series* (1978), p.1.

8 *Chapman*, 60 (1990), p.3.

and the Abbotsford. Mackay Brown reflected that, 'Some of the happiest hours of my life have been spent in these two poets' pubs...Never did the bird of poetry sing so sweet and true'.[9] In Sandy Moffat's iconic painting, *The Poets' Pub*, Mackay Brown is in the company of luminaries such as Norman MacCaig, Hugh MacDiarmid and Sorley Maclean. The John Barleycorn-influenced revelry of the Rose Street poets may well have been exaggerated but it can be regarded as one of Mackay Brown's personal falls.

Following nearly three decades of prohibition on Orkney, Mackay Brown recounted to his biographer Maggie Fergusson that when the Stromness Hotel reopened its bar in 1948 he went in, downed two glasses of beer, and was hooked. Those first glasses, he wrote, were 'a revelation; they flushed my veins with happiness; they washed away all cares and shyness and worries. I remember thinking to myself, 'If I could have two pints of beer every afternoon, life would be a great happiness''.[10] He was later to reflect in his memoir, *For the Islands I Sing*, that drink occupied more than 30 years of his life and writing, 'But it was a tarnished and a tainted glory, that brought me a good deal of anguish'.[11]

After graduation, Mackay Brown had toyed with a career in teaching, enrolling at Moray House teacher training college, just around the corner from the present-day Scottish Poetry Library in the Canongate quarter of Edinburgh. However, he was to fall foul of poor health, a consequence of the tuberculosis that had blighted his youth. Mackay Brown returned to Orkney

---

9   *Edinburgh Evening News*, 23 April 1983.

10 Maggie Fergusson, *George Mackay Brown: The Life* (2006), p.89.

11 Brown, *For the Islands I Sing*, p.72

soon after to live with his mother, Mhairi, a native Gaelic speaker. He converted to Catholicism in December 1960 at the age of 39.

Mackay Brown's first published poem, 'Prayer to Magnus', appeared in the *New Shetlander* in October 1946. In this poem, Mackay Brown was to visit some of the themes which were later to become central to his work. The name of Magnus is invoked as a prayer of renewal and realisation for the Orcadians. N D Garriock cited Mackay Brown's poem as being influenced by W B Yeats' trope of the man of action – the heroic Viking contrasted with the 'paler blood and softer bones' of contemporary islanders. In Mackay Brown's world, progress is seen as regress, particularly the lure of Scotland's cities for the island's young folk.[12]

Edwin Muir in his introduction to Mackay Brown's debut collection, *The Storm*, stated that he was 'impressed by something I can only call Grace', adding that Mackay Brown possessed, 'the gift of imagination and the gift of words; the poet's endowment'.[13]

Over time, the poet would experiment with his use of form. The constraints of three and four-stress lines were set aside as Mackay Brown's confidence grew in writing in free-verse. Kathleen Jamie wrote admiringly that he had a natural ear for the rhythm of free-verse: 'He had an excellent ear for all language'.[14]

Mackay Brown's second collection, *Loaves and Fishes*, was

---

12 *Chapman,* 60 (1990), p.3.

13 George Mackay Brown, *The Storm* (1955), 'Introduction'.

14 Brown, *The Storm and Other Poems* (2017), p.10.

published in 1959. It was championed by Edwin Muir who had sent a selection of poems to Hogarth Press. In this book, Mackay Brown was to rewrite or amend five of the poems that had originally appeared in *The Storm*. The reworking of poems was to become a pattern of Mackay Brown's work covering five decades of more than a dozen collections with publishers Hogarth Press, Chatto & Windus and John Murray. His collaborations included *Orkney Pictures and Poems*, with photographer Gunnie Moberg, and *The Martyrdom of St Magnus*, an orchestral work by composer Peter Maxwell Davies, which was the centrepiece of the first St Magnus Festival on Orkney in 1977.

Mackay Brown died in April 1996 at the age of 74. His biographer, Maggie Fergusson, wrote that, in the language of the sagas, he passed 'out of the story' with the final words: 'I see hundreds and hundreds of ships sailing out of the harbour'.[15]

---

15 Fergusson, *George Mackay Brown: The Life,* p.288.

PREFACE

Fiona MacInnes

George Mackay Brown

Well it wis George Broon fir a start. There wis none o that MacKay stuff. Or Georgie, thur wis wans that called him Georgie. He jist geed aboot an most o iss didna ken anything aboot the writin. Posh 'literary' folk came up fae Sooth and smelt of cologne. Nobody we kent wore cologne. Yi just hid yur smell. Mibbe the posh folk thought the MacKay bit made George Broon no so 'common'. Weel hids al aboot marketin is it no. He wis just wur George, makkan is laugh wi his mimickin o the folk that got above themselves (gawd meenisters an heedmesters were in fir it) or Stan Laurel, he cood dae him tae a tee. Then great long rantins o that owld borin poetry they got geed in the school, belted intae them they said. 'Infants 1&2' that photo. Us when we wur peedie craalin aboot among the brew bottles and the chantan and the singin. Sankey hyms warbling away like wan unholy congregation of my cup runneth over, an The Forsyte Saga on Sunday night telly. Best thing aboot George wis he always geed us a Selection Box at Christmas and telt us he had that many bairns he lost coont. We kinda believed him cause we wanted ti meet the bairns. 'Oh Oh, Ah'll hiv tae go' he wid say, 'Me bairns is waitin'.

GEORGE MACKAY BROWN (1921-1996)
BY ALEXANDER MOFFAT (TANKERNESS MUSEUM)

POETRY AND SHORT PROSE

Awaiting the Summer Walker
After R S Thomas

Morag Anderson

MacGregor her name, a Summer Walker
carrying baskets, bundles, and bairns
born on the banks of the Spey. Her father
a pearl-fisher who fell for a girl with indigo eyes,
waist-length curls—black as the cave she dwelled in.
When yellow blossoms on the broom they move west
though towns of smoke and slate, pitch willow sticks
and stretch bow-tents on the edge of my village.
She marks her year with songs and fairs, I mark
her coming by the colours on my loom.
She draws water to wash her rope of hair,
sleek as mermaid's tresses tugged from a stream.
Hidden in long grasses, I watch the sun settle
on her shoulders as day begins its end.
She is known for healing horses; soothing
red-eyed ghosts who stand at moonlit crossroads.
Taut and tense as an unplucked string,
I ask her to foretell my future; her fingers
slim and bare as a hedge in winter.
I taste the latent sweetness of wood-sorrel
on her breath as she leans in to say my name
will be scratched in neither stone nor clay.

Masks: A Zoom Conversation with George Mackay Brown

Aileen Ballantyne

The soup on the stove is carrot and onion;
open on the bookshelf, a mildewed *Selected Poems*:
for Masefield's Centenary '78 (price £5.99).
Today is GMB's turn. He looks out to sea,
his face still the same: *a face
that'd get a scone at any door.*

Surinder, his aide, stands behind him,
switches on the machine.
GMB, on the screen –
used to this now – finds it suits him.

He turns, puts the Basildon Bond writing pad aside;
it is one p.m: his five hours
'questioning the silence' completed.

He juggles his masks: loner, lover, drinker,
thrawn, agoraphobic, depressive,
kind friend, conversationalist, poet –
decides on the last three.

In close-up now, we see every detail:
forget,
all of it but this last mask.
None of it, none of it matters,
and we listen enthralled,

remote but connected.
He knows we are listening:
that he is not alone.

Notes:
1. George Mackay Brown: 'My other friend Surinder Punjya who does all my shopping and cuts my toenails and polishes my shoes – when he isn't studying Latin and Sanskrit scripts...I wish you could meet him: he's the nearest to a saint I've met so far'. Ron Ferguson: '...a face that would get a scone at any door', re George Mackay Brown. Ron Ferguson, *George Mackay Brown: The Wound and the Gift*, pp.351, 277.
2. The reference to John Masefield's centenary *Selected Poems* (1978) is from 'A Sea Poet, 6.7.1978', George Mackay Brown, *Under Brinkie's Brae* (2014), pp.156-73.

Strata

Gabrielle Barnby

Beyond Warbeth beach,
Hoy rises, back into clouds,
Cold streams from the Cuilags.

Snow packs tight into dykes,
Hurled hard between stones,
Ribboning road and furrowed hills.

A stone land, a place of geology
Without utterance, mark or stain.
Trace the name; be silent, be still.

Across shoreline gradient
Fragments wear thinner,
A pilgrim passes close to the edge.

Above, white birds cry the seasons
Among the cliff-fresh falls;
Each dark fault an active sign.

Old Red Sandstone and Stromness Flags
The deep reaches of creation,
While on the surface – bright yellow lichen blooms.

The Gate of the Kirkyard Rattles

Gabrielle Barnby

Warbeth beach, half a mile. The dykes either side of the lane are chalk-spattered with lichen. There is no cemetery sign, but I see the upright stones. From a distance some look like black shouldered mourners. Other stones wear tweed or glow gaudy like the cathedral. The more modern stones are hip-high, as if weathered by a contrary shorewards breeze. Older stones have monumental pretension, urns balance on pedestals while angels look on.

> An unknown bird sits
> waits for photograph in hope
> of identity

A line of surf breaks in the distance, energy dissipating in crosswise spumes over an unseen rock. Sheep are tearing hay from a circular metal feeder. It is the leanest time of year and the lambs are ready to come. The poet's stone is attracting lichen far more than others, and the carvings will soon be reclaimed, covered by life.

> Spring sun blares yellow
> on empty pierhead bench
> smiles await new guest

St Magnus Day, 1996

For George Mackay Brown

Pamela Beasant

Shadow on the stone
echoes the angular jut of your chin;
fleetingly, you are everywhere,
except in the box being lowered down

and it's hard to leave you there,
to not look after you, bring blankets
for the cold, and soup to nourish, to show
that you had made it to another spring.

Old men weave a spell of death,
tangle in it willingly,
drop from the end of a history
that tries to breathe, and can't.

This will be the day we start to endlessly repeat
by heart the litany of a book slammed shut.

God and Magnus, Island, Hamnavoe,
squandered a feast of images through
one life; took you, feather-light,
left us circling the gap.

Exposed on ancient contours,
pinioned by an inexorable sky,
on this St Magnus Day, we cry
for George, at Warbeth, where you lie.

I Can Still See You

Norman Bissell

I can still see you
striding out close to the wall
of the OFSL
that determined look caught
for all time by Oscar
and I understand why
you seldom left those tight flagstone streets,
the big city held few attractions
save one who lured many
a poet to her lair.

And I can see why
you felt at the centre of things
up there on your island
I feel that here
and have no wish to be anywhere else.
That first visit the Ness
was yet to be discovered
a mere glint in a dreamer's eye
but that feeling was there
at the Ring and the Brochs.

I well mind being telt aff
for climbing in the window
of the youth hostel one night —
but why did they lock us in?
And thon gull that squawked on deck

as Kenneth White read
Brandan's Last Voyage down below
then walking round the coast
and Gunnie stopping to give
us a lift back into town.

Then there was the time
I read *'For the islands I sing'*
at the start of my talk
at the Pier Arts Centre
and I realised that
Skara Brae had inside lavvies
long before the Romans.
But, you know, the great thing
you left behind was the chance
to see those islands
with your eyes.

A Wee Goldie

David Bleiman

> *He woke in a ditch, his mouth full of ashes.*
> George Mackay Brown, *Hamnavoe Market.*

Neilson stopped the Antabuse,
he spiralled through a case of Bells.
His colleagues called for his dismissal.

I used the old trade union tricks,
he saw the sense and took the package.
He drank it in a New Town basement flat.

I drove him down to Morningside
to detox in the ward. He joked —
let's try the Canny Man instead!

His wife had gone with both the girls,
he spoke of them each time we met.
I shook their black-gloved hands at Warriston.

Rogers was a veggie, ran marathons,
an intellect like liquid light,
a trenchant, troubled strategist of the movement.

We took a pint or three in Notting Hill,
pissed off the platform at Earl's Court,
then worked through freebie whiskies on the plane.

His knees went first and then the woman,
love of his life, for whom he'd left his wife,
and three beers became five, then nine.

I couldn't face the funeral in the west,
his daughter, widow and two exes.
Too late to stop his slide, I held my guilt at home.

Sinclair flashed across the globe,
from Rangers to Ramallah,
all knew him as the worker's friend.

To whet or maybe blunt his razor wit,
he took a drink – *jist a Guinness then
and och, Ah'll mebbe hae a wee goldie.*

So here we stand in rain, who stood our rounds,
at lunch set drinks up at his table –
the hall's stowed out, our mouths are full of ashes.

Beside the Oceans of Time

Helen Boden

i – *Cartography: 13 April 1996*

Hurled brittle bones
of early people or splints
from their familiar beasts

pieces of a broken pattern
these almost ink-blot islands lie
in spot-the-difference symmetry.

An anatomy of names
for flung shapes spun sunwise
from the vortex of Eday:

Westray, Pappay, North Ronaldsay,
Sanday, Stronsay, Shapinsay,
Gairsay, Wyre, Rousay, Egilsay

and back to Westray
by now a fragment less
a pebble displaced

as another wave crests

ii – *Good Friday in an Island: 10 April 2008*

St Margaret's Hope:
hailstorms, indigo sea -
an agreement

iii – *Weathering: 16 April 2021*

Imagining a coastline: round
the headwaters of the Leith,
sea-cliffs over Auchinoon,

Corston, Ravelrig & Kaimes.
Orcadian honeying of gable-ends
on Lothian steadings, on dykes.

Quarried basalt turned into
a roadside installation: stand-in
sea stack, substitute Brodgar.

St Magnus Day again
at the centre of the plateau scraped
by a glacial Water of Leith

into a credible Egilsay

On Being Pushed into Skara Brae

For George Mackay Brown

Colin Bramwell

One hand arrowed at my back
forces the step-off. I land on sand.
A cauldron of kelp thickens over
its fire like a question. Even at nine
I outsize the runetalkers. Grudgingly,
they open my space at the hearth. I do
not master their tongue, nor they mine.
Song is present as stone.

A ladder falls through space like a line.
I climb the wall of sand into now.
My brother is being scolded for
pushing me in. I forgive him, over
and over again, in the car back
to the tent. We sleep side by side.
One buried hand arrows up from below.
Stones sing into my spine.

Bear, Dancing

Niall Campbell

It wears the bracelet of the clamp, and dances,
awkward as a wedding guest; its fur
wetly dark with rice and milk–
         we have watched it,
swaying in the corner of the market,
beside the spices, its owner fat and sweating,
hand on the stereo.
         But now its stops,
exhausted and quiet, the crowd departs,
and sat there it finally dances, head
bowed to its huge chest, paws at its side,
huge, like my father, dancing in a stillness,
head nodding, his body still as evening.

Portrait of George Mackay Brown

Inspired by a photograph of George Mackay Brown
by Gunnie Moberg

_____

A C Clarke

Staunch as the sea-stacks that defy stormwinds
and the lash of the waves,
you turn your sea-grey eyes to the north, frowning
with concentration. What do you see?

The jut of your jaw a headland, the curve of your brow a hill,
you have grown into this land
like the ancient stones driven into turf at Brodgar.
Let Stromness be overrun

by frenzied tides as the sea rises higher and higher,
let a spasm in earth's gut
split the town from its moorings, set it adrift in the bay,
let the whole island plunge down,

a second Atlantis, your bones will not be parted
from their harbouring soil. And if
in centuries to come divers should sift the graveyard
for sunken treasures they'll find you there,

under your pink headstone, its *carved runes* green
with water moss, your writer's fingers
threaded by darting fish, your eyes no longer searching,
your smiling mouth *content with silence.*

Notes:
The italicised words are George Mackay Brown's own and are carved on his
headstone.

The Ocean of Time

In memory of George Mackay Brown

Stewart Conn

This elegiac sequence, written shortly after George
Mackay Brown's death while Stewart Conn was working
on a radio version of the novel from which it takes
its title, first appeared as a Christmastime tribute in
The Scotsman. The early volume, _The Year of the Whale_,
was published by the Hogarth Press in 1965. Erlend
Brown is George's artist nephew. Tam MacPhail ran
Stromness Books & Prints, and his wife Gunnie Moberg
collaborated with George on _Orkney Pictures and Poems_
(1996). Hopedale was his trusted friends Archie and
Elizabeth Bevan's house, in Stromness. Gypsy was a
black-and-white cat he regularly looked after (_Letters
to Gypsy_, 1990).

i

Hard to think your one-man
welcoming party has gone;
your prow-chin left
harbour, its voyage done;

your workroom window
facing out to sea,
once a source of light,
now a blind eye;

no handwritten note
pinned to your door
saying you'll be
back shortly.

The iron harpoon
you were given in the Year
of the Whale has found
a new home with Erlend.

ii

More and more your
friends miss you; this
the first winter
they'll be without you.

Yet your presence
is all-pervasive:
in Tam's book-cave,
Gunnie's magic lens;

night-tread from Hopedale;
scratch of pen, salt
on the pane; word-geese
massed on the skyline.

And as the mists clear,
a familiar figure
seen wraithlike
on headland and shore.

iii

Everyone's talk
so warming,
it's a shame
you can't join them.

Or simply
rock slowly
in your old chair,
Gipsy on your knee.

Rain blatters
at the window;
dark shapes
claw at the pane.

Over Hamnavoe,
a double rainbow:
vision and dream,
a perfect cradling.

iv

South of Yesnabay
a solitary seal-pup
seems stranded,
far from the ebb.

It belly-flaps
over the rocks,
ungainly till
it plunges

and reappears
riding the crest,

eyeing me from safety,
all muscular sheen.

Your life spent
in your element,
a dogged defiance
of surging forces.
v
Weaver of tales,
a spirit to match,
you caught the spirit
of these Islands,

merging emblem
and meaning, welding
'holy and carnal
in one flame'.

Fitting, in the hush
of St. Magnus,
to come across these
lines from your poems

in the key
to the west window:
'golden sun, wheat-
stalks, fishes'.

vi

I see you on a blue
bench by the pier
against a white wall,
all fisherknit jersey

and tangled hair,
eager as a boy
going to sea
for the first time.

Now in the longship
of the setting sun
your last journey.
Gannet and gull

on the cliff-edge squall,
as the fiery vessel
glides behind Hoy.
Darkness. A muffled bell

River Watcher

After George Mackay Brown's 'Beachcomber'

Laura T Fyfe

Monday I found a shoe –
curling and peat brown.
I left it there, washed up, waiting.

Tuesday a broken bough floated by.
Next week
it will be a raft of reeds, or ice.

Wednesday a half tub of bobbing oil.
I nodded my head.
The Forth was cold with memory spreading.

Thursday there was nothing. Dark
and swollen with silt.
Unmoving, the tide on the turn.

Friday I held an oyster shell.
Light gleamed on mother of pearl
the way sunrise shines on oceans.

Saturday a strange swirl in the water.
A seal raised her head,
blinked and drifted downstream.

Sunday I sit. Watch everything flow
away. The treasure in a river is not
in what it brings.

Beachcomber 2021

After George Mackay Brown

Magi Gibson

Monday, I find a bright blue rubber glove
Cast like a gauntlet on the sand.
Nature versus Man.

Tuesday, a perfect whorl of shell,
Shimmering shades of ocean, sand and sky.
I hold it to my ear. A mermaid hums a lullaby.

Wednesday. A flip flop. Yellow as a dying sun.
I cast it on the waves. It flips and flops
With the ease of a sleazy politician.

Thursday, I listen to the seals' song
And dream all night of lost loves
And drowned souls.

Friday. A trillion plastic particles
Sparkle on the shore. Jewels for fools.
The ocean roars her pain. Spits her ire.

Saturday, a lifejacket, orange,
Washed up from last night's storm.
Humanity sending out an SOS.

Sunday, I mourn a future sold
for a barrel of oil. The sky a darkening throng
of sharp-beaked, mean-eyed gulls.

Nae Rhyme or Reason

Jo Gilbert

Grunny's coupon curdles tae gargoyle, clockin the model
o a bizarre luikin een.
Nae rhyme or reason for at, she snaps, nae up for arguin –
a statement o fact.
Ma ain gaze hings aroon, teasin ideas oot like strings o
meltit cheese
expandin threids o possibilities, lingerin ower fit it mecht be.

Grunny's vitreous surety piques ma curiosity, her strict
binary has nae middle grun, it's iss wye or yon:

fyte/blaik
recht/wrang
loon/quine

Bidin sae blin tae onythin ootside yer ain purview's a mystery
tae me,
how kin she live in sic a narraw warld, withoot ony grey?
If aa could, aa'd peel aff her defences, fin oot fit warrants at
level o anger.
Bit naebody's brave enough tae cut sae deep, Grunny reacts
like an ingin, she'll spit – sting yer een an mak ye greet.

Caithness

John Glenday

Late May.
Rapefields in open blossom.

You pull into a layby
to savour that heady fullness

of yellow, staining the air
an inspissate blue –

far closer to ocean than sky.
And suddenly your way is clear:

no ship, no berth, no sail,
no family at the quayside

waving goodbye;
only a sea that will never

become a sea, and you
already stepping from the car.

Burns o Innertun

Yvonne Gray

i

it is silent -
        your water-song
                that welled
                        from the moor
            on Erne Toog
        where white-tailed
sea eagles soared

sotto voce it rises -
        the canon you wove
                in the Burn o Cringlegeo
                      and the Burn o Clook
            that sang in the spate
        that turned
the mill-wheel at Pow

it fades -
        the cadence that fell
            at Warbeth
                      past lead-runed rock
            and steeths
        where seaweed-gatherers
hung ware to dry

it lingers -
    the song that splurged
        over shore stones
            uttered syllables
      into Hoy Sound
    grew tongues
in the tides of the Atlantic

ii

when wind streams over the hill
    and funnels through the gully like water -

    when the torrent of kye
        hurtles between the banks

        purling backs that gather and seethe
           damned behind the gate -

when barley hisses
    and ripples like waves -

    when sparrows flurry in warm earth
        and spurt up dust like spray -

        when a curlew drifts to the field
           piping its water-flute song -

    when a snipe drums its airy bodhran
        and bubbles of sound well at dusk -

when an otter
        sinuous as a wave

        lopes through
                the dry stream bed

                nosing for the source
                                there

                and here
                                an echo

                or shadow
                        you linger

North of Troy

For George Mackay Brown

George Gunn

> *'Near the middle of the world was constructed that building and dwelling which has been the most splendid ever, which was called Troy.'*

from the *Prologue of the Edda* by Snorri Sturluson (1179-1241), translated by Anthony Faulkes.

1

I Bragi Boddason
testify to this
these kennings
runes carved on tongues
runes of fire
burning butterflies
on the foreheads
of the gold-keepers
the hall-watchers

2

Bragi cuts a rune

The Sea has a certain rhythm
seek it
understand it
go with it
& you will go far
he goes & dreams
of Helen

3

Troy is built

On Dunnet Beach
before the many Winters
was the mighty gap
Ginnungagap
which was cold with ice-wind
when this met the fire-wind
of Muspell
a man was formed
Ymir
father of giants

the sons of Bor
sons of stones
killed Ymir
some drowned in his blood
which became the Sea
his flesh the Earth
rocks were formed
from his bones & teeth
Ymir's skull
became the Sky

as the remaining sons of Bor
walked along Dunnet Beach
they came across two logs
storm-washed
from them they made people
a man called Ask
& a woman called Embla or Answer
on the stone of the blood-sea

they built a city

Troy

> *'So someone there was given the name Thor – and this*
> *means the ancient Thor of the Æsir, that is Oku-Thor –*
> *and to him are attributed the exploits which Thor (Hec-tor)*
> *performed in Troy. And it is believed that the Turks told*
> *tales about Ulysses and that they gave him the name*
> *Loki, for the Turks were especially hostile to him.'*
>
> from the *Prologue of the Edda* by Snorri Sturluson
> (1179-1241), translated by Anthony Faulkes.

4

The eruption had broken through the ice

The men stood at a distance
the women kneeled
beside their dead children
who lay on the frozen beach
like clubbed seals
still & questioning
eyes mouths wounds
dhu lochs of scarlet
seeped over the ice
& down into the sand
the foul stench of Fenrir
was on the wind

where asked the men
is the one called Thor
where is his power?
Where whispered the women

is the one called Hector
where is his skill in magic?

there were ten dead children
two brothers & their sister
buried under needless rubble
a boy & his cousin caught red fury
their laughter was over
a boy nearly a man
had three holes in his chest
a girl who felt the ravens claw
lay beautiful in her eighth year
a baby clutched her toy
& the blackness of armies
another boy lay face down
the back of his head open to the gulls
a girl who was always kind
offered also to the gulls

as Bragi tells it then
the women rose up
& one of them produced a vat
into which they all spat
one poured in honey
each gathered up
a frozen handful of scarlet sand
& set it into the vat
from this ice-hot sweet
salt blood mix
said Bragi
poetry is made

to the South Morven
covered by ice
shook & boiled
& reddened the sky
soon the eruption
had broken through the ice
Fenrir the world-wolf
sunk beneath the Cassiemire

the men gave thanks to Thor
for the volcano
& his thunder
the women wept into the vat
when Bragi told them
he was not Hector
they made me
drink from the vat
so I could tell of this
said Bragi

the men dug ten graves in the sand
the women laid their children down
above the high tide mark
the sea washed the scarlet clean
from the shore

5

Bragi speaks of the sea

Who can really understand the sea
not us who must live by it
not those surely who have never seen it
the sea is everything

the sea is nothing
the sea is perfect
we rowed over it from the broken land
to this land beyond the pine trees
to this empty place
which we have filled
with our memories
for there was nothing here
save for the whale
the seals & the occasional ice-bear
you may ask are we lonely
& I say no we are not lonely
& yet we are alone
at night the sky paints our story
in fire & flickering white beams
& then we know
all is well

my name is Bragi Boddason
the skald as they will have it
after me
is silence

Knap of Howar, Papa Westray

Mandy Haggith

A skylark above the stone age house
tells its version of history,
sermonising from its lofty pulpit,
a passionate speech from a high lectern.

At the Knap of Howar, words
from Trump and Johnson, Farage and May
seem so far away, so fickle, so fleeting.
What lasts?

A stone house for a family by a tidal sea.
A welcome from strangers.
Sky held aloft by a trilling bird.
Six thousand years of larksong and thrift.

Pinnie's Close

'A hundred years of rainfall', George Mackay Brown

Nat Hall

Below the stars, a high window,
          top of his world, minutes away fae Clouston's Pier.
The sea runs through the streets of
                    Stromness,
deep in the veins of
                    Stromnessians,
Knocking on doors,
               past the hotel...
Idyllic stones in
a sea-close,
          flagstones and turn of tides –
a hundred years of rainfall wash off its walls,
haily puckles, snowflakes or shine,
          stars in his sky; on
the hearing of the north wind,
clear-cut water runs on
his skin, drips off his
pen –
a hundred years of dancing kelp by the harbour,
          bench, boat station, where
the sea sticks on lips and souls,
          turning the water into verse –
gritting salt in his throat,
Pinnie's Close,

safe, as
        it held the key to the child,
high, shining stones after
              rainfall and ebbing tides.

Seekan back tae Rackwick

Simon W Hall

The pestilent East wind
quit its pitiless winnowing tae draa breath,
and in the lull, we won again – godless pilgrims -
tae Rackwick, the poet's valley.

Bejewelled Rackwick. Did we expect
tae find them changed:
the mountain, the wood, the ocean?
The poet turns his wheel.

Fae the summit o the Cuilags we surveyed
the gray mewling harrier below,
the aspen greetan intae the ravine o Berriedale,
pink sandstone wearing tae saalt o the sea.

And your mythos, George beuy,
that we had begun tae question
as Romish eccentricity, pagan irrelevance,
is here again in this valley, urgent and necessary.

Your tuskhar divides the paet bank,
curling the weet, dark pages,
revealing in the black slab
the glimmer o the papal ring.

And the fleet, green Christ
simultaneously running through
the Berriedale bracken, and
impaled there among the sweet white roses.

Though the wind rises again in the East,
your myth draas hidsael up, shakkan watter fae hids feathers
silver in hids beak, soaran oot ower the bay -
oot beyond the Owld Man, oot intae the forivver.

Mayburn Court, March 22nd 1996

Simon W Hall

Fae the ootside, the modest
cooncil hoose o the master poet
seems a monk's two-bedroomed cell.

Suddenly at the threshold
the iconic, troubled face;
gull-gray eyes, and the sad mooth.

But his jaw thaws tae its natural
shy-boy smile – welcoming me,
his thoosandth reader-pilgrim.

The lum draas; the embers lowe.
He dozes. Neither o us kens
he has drifted intae his final month.

(I canna see past the image
o that gizzened yole, aboot tae cast off
intae Hoy Soond.)

He luks oot, his eye drawn
doon close and pier
tae the peedie bit o sea

oot the gable window:
an acre o gray brine bristling,
beckoning in the March wind.

Dramman at the Nose o the Yard

Simon W Hall

August, early evening, at high
omniscient Mucklehoose,
perched on the peedie green neb
o pasture – the 'Nose o the Yard' -
that sniffs oot between the mountain
and the craig above the Pentland Firth,
I cam aroond the low, stone gable-end
(translated – I must admit – and a peedie bit
high mesael eftir a hot day on the Hoy Hills)
toward the westering sun oot ower the Atlantic,
thowts o strong drink crossing me mind
like red throated divers in flight,
when I met suddenly wae the sweet
black slap o pipe reek: and there he wis,
GMB, sittan waitan for me!
Duffel coat and biro laid aside,
pipe guffan, a tin mug o paetbank
whisky in his hand, and a gleam
in the clear, impish eyes – oblivious
tae the peedie bugger midgacks.

Beuy, I said, *It's so good tae see thee!*
Let me tell thee whit's been happenan
while thoo're been awey! Those fermers
and fishermen you ennobled? Weel,
most o them are still humble (but wan or two
did become money-grabbers and gilravagers

o the land and the seabed). The demographic
has lurched. The pasture and tilth are aal
satellite-mapped. And the stones and the brochs
are trampled by a million tourists. But here wae you
noo it's cheust possible tae believe that no aal o wur
culture's been thieved, misappropriated; some survives –
like hoo tae catch a spoot, or hoo tae mak clapshot
fae a frosted neep, or hoo tae navigate the roosts, or finnd
your wey safely home fae the Dwarfie Knowes. Jaas,
the sacred heart o Orkney's beatan still
noo that thu are back in Hoy again!

Whit whisky we drank! Whit yarnan we did!
Deep in wur cups as the stars chimed intae life
like peedie bells above the holy valley, watter
o life bringing us taegether again. Eventually,
there wis no gettan awey fae it, hid wis time
for bed. So we poured thee, George, golden spirit,
intae Glen's paet barrow, and wheeled thee
up the track tae Sylvia's, whar sheu wid watch
ower thee till dawn, while thoo dreamed the dreams
only a poet kens. *Goodnight, George beuy,*
I said, but only temporarily, *I love thee.*

Call o the Sea

Jenifer Harley

Oan the balcony
o a sea-lashed
stone-built inn
owerhangin the firth,
nowt but twa chairs fur company,
ma mind drifts wi the motion
an spectacle o the sea.

In the deep,
a plight o power struggles
swirl in constant rowin
forcin a gurglin gobble
tae suck in and belch oot
spirallin currents o frothin sprays
purgin the coast in worried rhythm.

As they come close
ruthless waves scour the shore
lik a covert SAS mission
inch by inch, sundried rocks
disappear—a crunch o sandy pebbles
tossed, gulped ower

then efter,
operations retreat, revealin
a salt-skimmed beach.

Seaweed zig-zags,
swampin the coastline
slitherin, strainin tae scale harbour walls,
bright wellies descend jumpin,
poppin, proddin wi sticks
faithers show off skimmin skills
tae excited bairns.

Memories stir
o beachcombin
fur redundant coals and shells
hoistit atop broad shooders
breathin in fresh briny air
feelin it nip ma face.

A pit oan ma coat wi the furry hood
an rubber boots.

Pneuma

Anne Hay

I watch the pink-bronze of a maple
rise and fall on the wind
rise and fall like a diaphragm.
Branches fan like bronchioles.

A whole day's plans
abandoned.
Sometimes the world
has too many voices.
An ache as familiar
as a favourite necklace.

Wind drops
the maple stills.
A soft outbreath.

Islander

W N Herbert

At midsummer midnight in Stromness I stare
out past some child's bear perched on the pier,
my father three months dead, you twenty years
or nearly, and neither nigh a toy's safe harbour.

At MacDiarmid's bidding word-storms sat on Whalsay
like good dogs by his epic-fuelled hearth;
MacLean's regret stoked lava-born Raasay
till Gaelic's stag stared from its molten wreath.

You grew a mountain from the sea's swung root,
and deepened in your winters that old trench
where tides may race between us till they drench,
then made a wreck-oiled island of your book.

MacCaig crofted on two lanes in the capital,
Rose Street for barley rig and Leamington for peat;
Graham from his Cornish caravan saw all
the canvas and the tin-tack waves he'd need.

A few treeless meadows awaited your text
amid the overtones of Rackwick where next
to scriptory herds, you sermonised to shoals
how poetry's an archipelago of souls:

While Crichton Smith found Murdo's maddened dance
in Callanish's storm-rewritten stance;
and Morgan, orbiting in Anniesland,
hung out a banner all Earth might understand.

This much more than anyone you could tell:
how the pen's tooth gnaws at age's keel
till the ferried whispers slow their reel
and strand us on a skerry of the self.

So why did I take so long to reach the island
these hailed as verse's haven? Because grief's gale
that gulls and claws us all until we fail
can in its random grace then drive us to dry land.

Andrina

Andy Jackson

In my imagination you come to me, to *him*,
to pile peat upon the smoking grate
and light the Tilley lamp when simmer dim

is smothered by the ash of night. It's late,
and spume is blowing off the loch,
a demon frothing at the mouth. I wait

but there is no sound now save the clock
whose hands sweep by in retrograde,
about-facing me as I hunker in my broch

of shame. All these years, and I'm still afraid
of you and what you know: everything
I know and more, the cruel games I played,

the plain girls I kissed while worshipping
their older sisters, jokes I told on friends
in fear of being joked by them, the ring

I placed on my own fat finger. This will end,
must end, with an islander's death, a birth
in retreat, as my deeskit body transcends

itself and is ingested into the sea-black earth,
leaving only the bobbing jetsam of my life-song
to drift beyond the Swelkie to the open firth,

and the ocean which knows no right or wrong.
Andrina, my own unspeaking Shibboleth,
I steered my boat toward the fog for so long,

yet we were separated only by a single breath.
You wear my shroud of words, my hair, my skin,
hiding in plain sight till rising out of death,

more than the momentary ghost of my kin,
and if you had knocked, I would have let you in.

Dark Plastic

After George MacKay Brown's 'Beachcomber'

Caroline Johnstone

Monday I found picnic leftovers -
Macro-plastics, micro-plastics.
The sea threw them back to me;
a slow danse macabre.

Tuesday, I crunched through
the time and tide of sea glass,
the crackle of crisp packets, dead balloons.

Wednesday spews an aftermath of oblivion;
cans and bottles – six pack rings.
Mermaids' tears have silenced mermaids' voices.

Thursday, there is never nothing to find.
I ran past a haul of ghost gear –
fishermen's gloves and nets and bait boxes.

Friday, sand spills from filled nappies, face masks,
neatly tied dog-waste bags.
Saltwater tears pour for next generations.

Saturday I closed my eyes to crows
picking over upturned crabs and oil-drenched gannets,
the slow death of seals strangled in nylon.

Sunday. I clutch a Rosary of dark plastic –
a hopelessness impossible to count.
What's hell? The unexploded bomb
for a child to stand on.

Holds off the Sky

After 'The Finished House'

Marjorie Lotfi

What is a house, but a borderline -
bodies we love huddled shoulder
to shoulder around a wooden table,
waiting for a hot ladle of soup,
the buttered heel of bread.
A beaker of water sits between us,
last drops refilled from the leaking
tap that keeps time like a clock.
Above, the roof holds off the sky
of possibilities, with its chance
of rain and its chance of sun, while
the warmth of the stove is a tether
to the stone floor under our feet.
Here, it is always us against them,
those beyond the door.

Licht Bringer

In memory of George Mackay Brown

Christine De Luca

Purest licht syin
trowe century, solstice:
a history unfowldin
but rarely revealed till
he read dem der runes
an telt dem der tales.

Aerliest settlers
makkin der biggins;
dan jarls wi langships
– a wirld o farfarin;
an saints wi der kirks,
der crosses an altars.

Dan lifters o creels
an a man at da maa
cuttin a swaar fur
da bread an da ale;
an da wife at da ferm
wi maet fur dem aa.

Lö ta da callyshang:
a glisk at da past i da
soonds o da cadence
fae aest an fae wast,
dat lilt i da laand
an a shörmal dance.

Light Bringer

In memory of George Mackay Brown

_____

Christine De Luca

Purest light straining
through century, solstice:
a history unfolding
but rarely revealed till
he read them their runes
and told them their tales.

Earliest settlers
making their buildings;
then jarls with longships
– a world of farfaring;
and saints with their churches,
their crosses and altars.

Then lifters of creels
and a man at the reaping
cutting a swathe for
the bread and the ale;
and the woman at the farm
with food for them all.

Listen to the hubbub:
a glimpse at the past in the
sounds of the cadence
from east and from west,
that lilt in the land
and a tideline dance.

Dìleab an Stoirm

Marcas Mac an Tuairneir

> 'Sand-inundated archaeological sites are found in many
> areas of coastal Scotland, including the western and
> northern islands. The most famous of these is Skara Brae
> on the Orkney island of Mainland. This Neolithic Age,
> World Heritage Site was exposed in 1850 when coastal
> erosion uncovered the seaward-facing portion of the site.'

Daniel H Sandweiss and Alice R Kelley
(*Annual Review of Anthropology*, 2012)

Geamhradh 1850 – ràith nan stoirm,
agus dà cheudnar nan righe ron adhlacair,
dhùisg sibh co-dhiù nur n-iarlach eileanach,
agus an t-iongantas, ro sgàil reòthach na sùla.

Bu raoic na cruinne-mhàthar a chur crìth mun talamh,
an cnoc air ais-rùsgadh
      mar phlaosg
          cnòtha
              chruinn
              agus ùir-bhreathan air an taisbeanadh.

Le ur corragan, dh'fhidir sibh clàbar
o bheàrnan na clachaireachd,
gus an glanadh le sàl is bùrn
is cuidhteas fhaighinn
de dh'eabar aoise.

Nur dèidh,
bhris tonn-mhillidh clann-daonna –
mobhsgaid,

      creach,

            trèigsinn,

                  mus do nochd cuid o Dheas,

                  chìtheadh luach tobhta gun mhullach.

Notes:
The poem relates to the discovery of Skara Brae, a Neolithic settlement on Mainland, Orkney, and the great storm that ravaged Scotland which unearthed the settlement.

The Legacy of a Storm

Mark Spencer Turner

> 'Sand-inundated archaeological sites are found in many
> areas of coastal Scotland, including the western and
> northern islands. The most famous of these is Skara Brae
> on the Orkney island of Mainland. This Neolithic Age,
> World Heritage Site was exposed in 1850 when coastal
> erosion uncovered the seaward-facing portion of the site.'
>
> Daniel H Sandweiss and Alice R Kelley (*Annual Review of
> Anthropology*, 2012)

Winter 1850 – the season of the storms,
and two hundred laid out before the undertaker,
you awoke in your island jarldom
to a wonder, through the frosty glaze of the eye.

It was mother nature's roar that sent shockwaves through earth,
the knoll peeled back
      like the husk
           of a nut,
                rotund,
                and the soil strata manifest.

With your fingers, you quit
the stonework's fissures
of their mire, to wash
away the sediment
of the ages with
sea-water and
rain.

In your wake,
broke waves of human wreckage –
incompetence,
plunder,
neglect
until the advent of a man from the south,
to ascertain the worth in a roofless ruin.

An Dìleab

As dèidh Julio Cortázar, airson George Mackay Brown

_____

Pàdraig MacAoidh

Nuair a chaochail do mhac anns a' Chuan a Tuath,
a chorp dealrach sa mhuir reòthtach,
bha thu nad bhreòig nad leabaidh,
do shlàinte ro bhrisg airson na fìrinn

agus nuair a thill e chùm an sgiobair
an ad aig' air a cheann, agus air a spot
rinn e sgeulachd dhen ghlaoic balaich ud
a bhris a chas far chosta Nirribhidh

's a bha a-nis am measg nan Lochlannach,
a' fàs reamhar, a chas a' fàs làidir.
Sgrìobh thu cairt-puist dha nad làimh iomluath
agus thàinig freagairtean siùbhlach:

cairt – 's an dèidh greis – litrichean, clò-bhuailte,
le gach bàt'-iasgaich, mu na cothroman
a bh' ann an sin: obair, beartas,
's mu dheireadh thall bean agus clann,

àrd 's bàn ri taobh taigh-ghil sgiobalta ghrinn.
Adhbharan do-dhiùltadh an aghaidh tillidh.
Agus ged a tha thu fhèin ann an Cladh Bharabhais
bliadhnaichean a-nis, 's an sgiobair cuideachd,

's a h-uile duine riamh a bha eòlach air do mhac,
tha na litreachan fhathast a' leantainn,
ginealach an dèidh ginealaich eòlaich,
ag inns' na breige a chumas a' dol sinn.

The Legacy

After Julio Cortázar and for George Mackay Brown

_____

Peter Mackay

When your son died in the North Sea,
his body radiant in the freezing water,
you were in your bed, a cracked vase,
your health too fragile for the truth

and so when he returned the skipper
kept his hat firm on his head and on the spot
made up a story about the bloody stupid boy
who broke his leg off the coast of Norway

and was now among Vikings
growing fat, his leg getting stronger.
You wrote postcards in your wandering hand
and got speedy, restless replies –

cards and then letters, typed,
with the season's fishing boats, about the chances
there were there: work, money,
and, after a while, a wife and children,

tall and fair against a neat white-house,
bog standard, unanswerable ties.
And though it's years now you're in
Barvas cemetery (the skipper too,

and all who remembered your son)
the letters keep on their to and fro,
generation on knowing generation,
telling the lie that keeps us going.

Mangurstadh

Hamish MacDonald

Drawn to the brink
of these time-battered crags
to Europe's last outpost
before Atlantic desolation.

Stalked by those
black ravens of Memory and Thought
it felt like Mangurstadh could lift you up
or drag you to its terrifying depths
as the white fulmar passed
a fleeting emissary of hope.

We found the primitive bothy perched on its ledge
like some monastic cell
where internal struggles had been wrought out
at the world's end
invading its dank air with the warmth of our stove
the aroma of frying square slice and hot sweet tea.

Finding a foothold
in remote and treacherous places
on the road back the eagle hung on January winds
behind me Mangurstadh
before another day.

The Camera Lies

Fiona MacInnes

She is the background filler
Element of another's earnest composition for
Tonal balance required
Walking into a slow shutter speed
That dull day
A street too empty maybe?
She pushes a double buggy
Trudging where?
Into another's image to become
Anonymous in the Scotsman
Behind the man they all know
One ground down
Prozac numb mother

Camera cajoles, clicks
He shifts and shot done
We both knew it was a moment
When he was between our world
And theirs'
As she passed
The exchange of nods said it
In words unsaid across the divides
That only us
Of this difficult place
Can understand

A Reply to the Poet

Ross MacKay

I am here now, troubling the pool of silence.
It's whispish edges evading my soft fingers.
I imagine your hands were rough,
With a tight grasp.
A weathered craggy landscape
Furrowed and cracked along the edges.

My uncle's hands were working hands.

He had a farm and each year we would burn back the heather
Flame and man.
Beating and thwacking
And fighting the wind.
Hard working the heat
Till the landscape strewn with ash
Was fresh again.

And you held your pen, snug, like a leather beater.
Thudding the noise into submission
And when all was done.
There was nought
but refreshed silence, which I hope to one day catch.

Portobello Beach

Rob A Mackenzie

The tide is in, and here's the haar
        go sad or sweet or riotous with beer
but still, they're licking ice-poles on
the shingle, stripped to their underwear
        despite the pincering frost,
ready to welcome another year of stone
by diving headfirst.

Easter weekend and empty vessels
        go sad or sweet or riotous with beer
line up with open gobs of sand
to swallow the insubordinate drizzle:
        breaking news, the same
illusions and conspiracies, the underhand
shifting of blame.

It must be the summer of polka dot pink
        go sad or sweet or riotous with beer
and upturned stracciatella cones;
the only solution is to drink
        until the sadness lifts
wave by wave by wave by wave, and soon
finds itself adrift.

The fish are battered for the deep-fat fryer
       go sad or sweet or riotous with beer
the sunbathers measure the depths
they'll keep within. Autumn flares
       scarlet in the sky;
tomorrow will be too cold to take a breath
on either land or sea.

Notes:
The line 'go sad or sweet or riotous with beer' is from George Mackay Brown's
'The Old Women'. The form is borrowed from his poem 'The Laird'.

Beyond the Swelkie

Jim Mackintosh

i

Sleet glimmers. Then a cowled steely darkness
blocks the winter dim. In his godly hand
a box of cinders – each grain named in sermon.

The plough waits, driven into the heavy dreel,
drift nets hushed in the slump of empty deck,
only the bait hooks stay sharp in defiance.

The priest marks foreheads, seeks out reluctance
in the eye if one dares to be offered up – nothing.
And clasped knuckles whiten from mussel blue

as the plough opens shoulders catching the stride
and the nets unravel on the pull of deepening swell.
The fold of Agnus Dei return to their darg – grateful.

ii

Old truths console, they do not waver in new language:
looking beyond, counting lives passing, the weight
of history still strapped to silent backs, buckle-hefted

seeking precious air, an inhale offering freedom
from pounding strife, of blackened hours choking
quarried days after dying days under scaffolded sky.

We seek solace carved in soil: peace to stop and know
the seasons will appear again, precious quartered veins
unfolding elements of our struggles, weather-wept,

waiting the rub of innocence. Even in these driven lands
seeds of hope still await release from blistered oppression
scarred by the distant toothless clinging to crooked folly.

iii

On the best days, our dreams find comfort on the back shore,
free from hungry tides, they hold soft on buttressed dunes
Under a bare bone tree, deaf to the siren's cry a child counts

time in the wind's catch of machair whose sweet honeycomb
of nature's direction unravels away from the priest's stare.
I look to silence-gatherers, praying for the child to take its dream

Barefoot and safe from the debt-assured knuckles of scaffold,
clothe it in textiles of knowledge, seek new dominions safe
from poisoning influence and carve new words in the old runes.

Uncork peaceful anticipation. Polish bright glass. Drink new dawns.
Out of ploughed words and broken vows know all this to be true –
from stack of peat, on urgent seas and here, far beyond the swelkie.

Orcadia's Continent

Paul Malgrati

when the buttered bannock over Hamnavoe
shares tray with St Malo's croissant de lune

when the tipsy laird fae Tankerness reddens
in a tchin-tchin of Nuit-St-George

when sunset oats alight on Kettletoft
and toast a millefeuille of tapsalteerie glee

I and my love will wake to fair isles on a plate
breaking fast late ere the hour of landing

Snow on the Shingle

Marion McCready

> '*The shore was cold with mermaids and angels.*'
> George Mackay Brown

We woke up to a white-out; the street tippexed over
like a huge mistake corrected in a single stroke.

Yet the polished leaves of our garden shrub,
its glistening jade, emerges intact untouched
except for tiny blossoms of powdery snow
  cupped in its shiny green paws.

There's snow on the shingle – all the way down
  to the very fringe of the Clyde.

Large pebbles and the chalk outline of a body
of seaweed protrude, occasional clumps
of dying stalks of seagrass scratch at the air.

The shore was cold with mermaids and angels.
Though we did not see them, they left footprints,
  tailprints, wingprints.
They left ice-sparkles, blizzard-breath, they left
mementos, mid-winter souvenirs of their presence.

The snow is their shed skin; it will not last.
But for now we stare into the bright gallery stretched
out before us; a gathering of light resting across

the long shingle that will soon melt then float off
into the air and follow us around like gulls
throughout the rest of the year.

Beachcombers

After George MacKay Brown

Beth McDonough

Monday I wanted a rub of mermaid's purse,
found none. My son hauled oarweed in a crackle-flag.
He threw it well out to reach for its boat.

Tuesday a half-gab clappy-doo, purpled and grey,
soon dulled in my hand. He twisted olive wrack
rosaries. Dropped at the high tide mark.

Wednesday slipped in skimming slates.
A fluted rim of Delft, collected for a friend.
His a fray-end fishing rope, unravelled. Left.

Thursday gave us both damp socks, tramped too near
the edge. This I tholed, but dreamed up teuchat storms.
He shed his boots. Traipsed on.

Friday totted both my pockets, added in
one stopper, and three-lettered frosts of glass.
Between his fingers, he chafed sea lettuce into skin.

Saturday kicked a half-embedded tyre, outstared
a crone's glare gnarled in driftwood. He tossed her
into marram's scything heart.

Sunday sifted sand through that disregarded Sabbath.
We took our findings home to cut stem scents.
His rucksack poured out spare clothes, nothing more.

Gorse Bushes

Jane McKie

Speaking in the language of spine and prickle, they announce
a fighting beauty. Blooming in winter, endurance stiffens
their stems, makes of them a company of earthbound archers.
Blooming in the last snows, 'Where is the sun to anoint
the suns of our petals?' In spring, a controlled explosion
of yellow hedgelings – spiky flourishing – better than a mine
of gold. And on summer cliff tops even the waves envy
the hi vis costume of skirts and spurs unfurling scent
sweet enough to douse the stink of weed; even the sky
is charmed by the hum and honey of their bristling seas.

The Poet
For JN

_____

Hugh McMillan

When asked, the poet could not
remember the names of her books,
in fact could not remember there
were any books at all, but sat down
and hand wrote from memory on

tight foolscap seven poems including
one several pages long. You see
she explained, you see, Mr ...
Dear, dear man, my memory
is not so good and I have been

called frail but It's very strange but
when I recall those days in
Muirkirk which means the church
on the moor, I see things quite
clearly, and these poems which

I am sending you are like that:
winter scenes and beasts and auld
fowk and bonny lassies – I wrote
about them in the language of the
people. And here they are now, always.

Silence

Julie McNeill

No more music now,
not a note shall flow
from that small house at Yesnabay
just south of Skara Brae,

a silence now at Sandwick
tucked in and bedded down
amidst the coastal cliffs
bricks built up like sea stacks

a shelter there in Stromness
from wind-crashed waves
from the rugged, wild, enchanting
and the impossible to tame.

A pause, here
for stories,
for humour
and for drams.

As birds of every colour
circle overhead,
words wash
and rush like rapids
through our
reeling heads

as we do our best
to content ourselves
with silence.

No Beaches to Comb

Victoria McNulty

We lay wet. Weekend rummaged a Saturday
willowed fingers walked a
soft smudge sunken barrel.
The dawn rain weight of
our brows salt sodden
your hair moonlit grey and oranges.

We ignited. A carry on a
a fevered fervour. Spanish
flu marooned us in this doldrum ship.

We painted it acrylic. It was
Emerald washed, whisky wreaked.
We loved it until the last
voyage floated up, hour after day and month.

We broke bread and soil. Toiled at
home. Dirt hands marvelled the
Earth as if it was The Kame.

*

Should I never ponder what's
Come before me in this tiny carve of Heaven?
This months long, blink second. A
face splash dream, you'd wash me out to Sea.
In this city I only comb your rib chest
heavy plundered with
oils slick dissatisfaction. I found a
blessed bounty thousand
there in you. A tarnished shimmering gold.
Believe in me as I clutch these coins.

Writing

Andrew Motion

1

Doctors in London told you: live,
which was a sentence of sorts
and meant I wanted to stay put
day and night at your bedside
like a ghost writer poised to turn
rough ideas into perfect sense.
But your life was no longer mine
to make a tricky move like that,
so I said I'd be in touch. Then left.

2

For Stromness as it happened.
I had written words for Peter
Maxwell Davies to set to music,
but with the first rehearsal done
put them behind me and strayed
outside into the light wondering
should this really be dark now?
My watch was saying one thing
and exhausted seagulls another.

3

This was way back in the days
when I worked for Chatto and
Windus, where I took on George
Mackay Brown as my author
only to be told he was dying.
But we did correspond at least,
him with a wind-blown script
that as far as I could make out
had grown as curly as his hair.

4

Whale roads and roofless crofts,
a tin bucket caught by the wind
and blown through an empty yard
with a circular trundling sound:
these entered his needle's eye
and poured through into mine -
not to mention the British fleet
sunk by the Brits themselves
to keep the Germans at bay.

5

Such damage we do to make
our floating selves feel safe.
By now I was holding a thread
of mist as if it might lead me
out through the labyrinth
of interchangeable lights
and along the coastal road
from Stromness into the wild
and George for old time's sake.

6

Green wheelie bins on the terrace
opened and closed their beaks
in intermittent gusts. So much
for the world in his window!
More gulls I did see, however,
posting themselves like letters
between stones of the harbour wall,
their pages blank that morning
if morning is what it was.

Solastalgia

Duncan Stewart Muir

That summer, after they sold the farm
and with it the hill, the quarry, the hazel
woods – an archaeology of middens scattered
among its roots – we gathered

in Kilmeny Graveyard to put John Dewar
to rest. How do you measure the magnitude
of loss? In simple acres, hectares, demesne?
In feet of loam? Or in memories and acts:

the moments of time that condense upon
a landscape, upon a mind. Winnowed
from the noise. Beyond that ancient dyke
lay the Rozgas' meadows, the cold, quick Sorn

her pools of speckled trout and stony fords
into which I'd fished and fallen more times
than I'd care to count. The flat-topped
dùn, where I'd rest and gaze out over

the valley, the sleeping giants of The Paps,
the forest of Daill, Ballygrant Woods
and the buzzards twisting up in the sky.
And I saw myself as the land

once knew me – a skinny boy in an oilskin
coat, air rifle over the shoulder, game
bag overflowing, belt festooned
with kill – brace upon brace of warm

limp rabbits hanging like saddle bags
from my slight frame. It was that same boy
who sculpted John Dewar's hands from clay
for his Higher Art portfolio, who helped

collect the eggs from his Houdan hens
and who sat in the corner of his hearth,
mirroring his silence, as the women talked.
But I stood by his graveside as a man

scattered soil in my turn as we gave
John to the land, that earth which birthed
these hills and fields and rivers, these sombre
men and women – all holding drams aloft.

Three Winter Poems

For Jenny

Donald S Murray

The Christmas Mermaid

It was a glow
that sent her out one December night,

Saturn, Jupiter conjoining,
merging into a strong light

near the horizon.
She saw its beam reflecting on her skin,

believed it might be the snow's sparkle,
scattered south on wind

blown in from the Arctic.
But when she tried and failed

to brush this clean,
she realised that, somehow, fish-scales

had silvered thighs and calves.
Soon tail and fin

appeared and she slipped
away on Christmas Eve, dipping within

the chilly waters of the bay.
We haven't seen her since that time,

our Christmas mermaid, Yuletide selkie,
apart from a beam that shines

from rocks and skerries, dark sea-stacks,
and we mourn how we have lost her,

how she never will come back.

A Dove at New Year

It was a sign that made them wish to leave
their homeland – the arrival of the white dove that appeared
among seabirds surrounding them on New Year's
Day. It signalled a beginning, a chance to breathe

after ages wearing the tight gag which had long confined
lips and thought upon the island,
the prospect of waking one fine morning to stand
upright on another shoreline, find

new songs to stir both throat and tongue
and discover, too, different patterns for their flight
like that bird which had appeared within their sight
and taught sounds and rhythms, granting them a sense
that there were other places to which they might one day belong.

An Island Christmas

After a close neighbour had taken ill,
my grandparents took in her child near December's end.
(They never called it Christmas,
seeking instead to pretend

it was just another wind-chilled winter's day.)
But those who lived nearby came to see them, slipping by
hens clucking round the manure-heap,
cattle curled up in the byre

at the entrance to the blackhouse,
visiting the child sleeping near the flames
at the centre of their home.
They all brought scones and milk when they came.

And prayers too, the hope a mother sick a few doors
down would lift that child again,
her health and strength miraculously restored.

Small Isles

Hamish Napier

Eigg is an old moon of Jupiter
Plucked from its orbit
By the mighty hand of Rhum,

Whose fingers enclose
The dark fortunes
Of her rugged palm.

Canna is a rabbit
Cautiously sniffing
In the shadows of Trallval.

Muck is fossilized trawler
Surfaced in the sound,
Forever bound for Mallaig.

The great dragon of Skye
Swishes her tail of Aird
As she takes flight for St Kilda.

The arrow of Ardnamurchan fires West,
Narrowly missing the tips of Coll and Barra Head
To strike the open Atlantic.

The voice of Inverie
Pulls in all the breath of the Sound of Sleat
And soars to the highest note on the summit of Ladhar Bheinn.

Fear a' Bhàta – Cèilidh Buan

A' cuimhneachadh air Ali 'Beag' MacLeòid, Ach' na h-Àirde

Màiri Anna NicUalraig

Fhir a' bhàta, ri beul fàire,
Dùsgadh gàire bhith aig an stiùir,
Sruth na stiùire air do chùlaibh,
Romhad reul-iùil gach port is dàn.

Sgeul ar là-sa, an-dè 's a-màireach,
Ghabh thu 'n dàn dhuinn, ghabh thu 'n ruidhl',
Cala sàbhailt' aig ceann do là dhuit,
Gum biodh an cèilidh an còmhnaidh dlùth.

Gach buille-dannsa leis a b' annsa,
Gach sèist is òran bh' air bilean gràidh,
Guth nan daoine, caithream ciùil bhuaith',
Len còmhnaidh gàire is lasair sùl'.

Sgeul ar là-sa, an-dè 's a-màireach
Ghabh thu 'n dàn dhuinn, ghabh thu 'n ruidhl',
Cala sàbhailt' aig ceann do là dhuit,
Gum biodh an cèilidh an còmhnaidh dlùth.

The Boatman – Everlasting Cèilidh

Remembering Ali 'Beag' MacLeod, Achnahaird

Mary Ann Kennedy

Boatman in the dawning,
Laughter wakened at the helm,
The rudder-wake behind you,
Before you, the guide-star of every tune and song.

Our today story, yesterday and tomorrow story,
You sang the song for us, you played the reel,
Safe haven for you at the day's end,
Let the everlasting cèilidh always be near.

Every dance-beat in which to revel,
Every chorus and song on darling lips,
The voice of the people in his harmony,
Ever a laugh and spark in the eye.

Our today story, yesterday and tomorrow story,
You sang the song for us, you played the reel,
Safe haven for you at the day's end,
Let the everlasting cèilidh always be near.

Notes:
Ali 'Beag' MacLeod – fisherman, accordionist, Còigeach Gaelic speaker and
beating heart of a community – passed away in January 2021.

Leaving the Island

Stuart A Paterson

Sitting on the bench, peering out to sea,
I'm sure you don't see Arran but
Ward Hill, the headland of Orkney
or Graemsay cut

cleanly through a mystery of tides
rolling always back to one day,
a tall lifeboatman by your side
and trawlers heading back safe to the bay
till Skara Brae

reveals itself as the Firth of Clyde
and a soft-spoken son with no sea
in his hair is standing by your side
waiting patiently

The girl from Hoy will remember, rise
and slowly turn to take an arm,
a different island in your eyes
and years of calm...

not huge horizons brimming with black,
a wake of widows, an empty chair
at table-head where he would sit
when he was there.

You say you'll not look out the window
to Arran when it's rough, prefer
a quiet prayer for the boys. Hard to outgrow
the feeling of stepping from shadows
where islands were.

Warbeth Walk

Nalini Paul

The air is thick
and quickens your breath
foam rushes like blood.

What's death?
Tombstones, planted bookmarks.
Salt rubs the wounds of letters.

Your feet push back the earth.
Legs spring like flight.

Oystercatchers pose on granite.
Blue light washes the fields.

So live for the fear of drowning in seascape
the end of words –
the black-and-white forking of tongues.

To speak like the raven
or sing like the curlew
feasting on what the shore offers.

To plunder deep into liminal space
for fish-meat and sustenance.

What's grace?
A lapwing song in a dark field.

An empty stomach
filled with the smell of seaweed
and cattle.

The curve in the road
where you listen for starlings...

You climb the last hill
walking backwards from the sea.

Then the wind whips you round
to the orange-glow windows of home.

Ambergris

Louise Peterkin

> *'The shore was cold with mermaids and angels'*
> 'Beachcomber' – George Mackay Brown

A week's worth of wanting, the oesophageal
pull, the stomach swag: a wolf's worth,
stitched

once filled with boulder to an adequate degree,
the ire of it, all that cold shoulder
sickening

vanishes when I glimpse you
idling outside the kirk with Sally-Anne and Phoebe,
one leg

scratching the other –
a brief ballerina in the Sunday sun.
Your arms are flecked with delicate yellow.

I swallow my hurt when you laugh at me.
Wastrel, they say. Lazy.
But what the sea spews up,

the whale spewed up –
sometimes
from time to time, ahhhh look hardly

ever. One day I will be lucky.
I detonate the bladderwrack with my boot,
wrangle my grey sack, wretched

with water. For what? The earwax globe
that mimics stones
and stony malformed babbies.

The beak of the bird is bound in the bile
and hums like a sarcophagus;
it is gold,

myrrh, frankincense.
On my knees on the shore
I'll cradle it – I,

the fool who followed in the footprints
of wise men
with holes in their pockets.

The Lit Room

In memory of George Mackay Brown

_____

Sheenagh Pugh

There was a flat
on a long street by the sea,
a room, scarcely lit,

a head of clay,
sunken-eyed, cheekbones hollowed,
a memento mori

for the face that glowed
from the shadows: so gaunt, so mobile.
There was a word

someone let fall,
that filled him, all of a sudden,
with light. A vessel

of ware so thin,
the wine shone through. Light leaks
into the ocean

when the clay cracks,
into the dark. Who notices
if the street lacks

one lamp, one face?
These days, the room is empty
of shadows,

well-lit, tidy.
There is a flat, on a long street
by the sea....

Archipelagos

John Quinn

Norse dyed, soft as Scots smirr
the voice rolls across decades
gifting word and verse, archipelagos of
vision and memory, a thousand Orcadian things.

The beachcomber heckles fibres,
the warp and weft of lives less ordinary
of teeming tides and spendthrift sea.
St Magnus inhabits the wind.

Hamnavoe has every market within,
agora, bazaar and souk in a colder climate,
diurnal detritus, and ineffable presence
of an Orkney girl with Afro hair.

Unsighted yet insightful
the travelling bard gets in and gets out
playing music beyond the land I know,
seer of a future not his own.

Hawks were Kes and Ted Hughes before.
This one is visceral educating
in a way Google does not.
One day I hope to pray on Lamb Holm.

The Wound and the Gift

Larissa Reid

You stand facing west,
Scanning the horizon
For white horses and angels.
The wind courses the lines on your face
And your eyes dance with the colours of the sea.
We're here to rub salt in the wound,
We're here with a gift of stolen time,
We're here with our gloved fingers intertwined;
Caught between a diamond cut for firelight
And a slice of that storm
Out in the broken green distance.
Our veins are shot through with silver,
As we move to shelter
In the lee of the broch,
With all the fragmented souls
That wheel with us here.
You are my wound and my gift;
And I will bend the world
To walk with you,
Scoured by sea spray and sand crystals,
Selvedged by the running tides.

Khyber Pass

Olive M Ritch

A good neighbor – we leave each other
to our privacies. And I do not get involved,
or gawp, when her brother, who lives with her
and who rarely leaves the house,

stacks chairs, tables, chest of drawers,
and sometimes a broom, outside,
on the lane, for everyone to see.
When my neighbour

                        returns home
from work, she takes the furniture
back into the house, closes the door,
and all seems normal again.

Notes:
Khyber Pass is a lane in Stromness. The line 'A good neighbor – we leave each other to our privacies' is taken from 'A Warm Day' by the 2020 Nobel Prize winning poet, Louise Glück.

A Fatal Blessing

James Robertson

> *'One senses a growing coldness – the coldness of people who have received the fatal blessing of prosperity.'*
> George Mackay Brown, 1970

Let us give thanks for what we have been spared;
the sheets of sweat that were never on our backs;
the blisters that did not rise on our fingers;
the scars and grain of toil that our bodies do not bear.

Let us rejoice that our tongues now speak in unison;
that every prejudice has been exposed and banned;
that old, misguided instincts have been driven off
the cliff of knowledge. Let us salute our public righteousness,

and the privacy that keeps unwarranted distress at bay.
The blood of what we eat is not on our hands; outer walls
shield us from the worst of weather, while inner ones
support the weight of worlds that open to us at a click.

We are not cold. Far from it. We are warm and safe,
and glad not to live in former times of aching labour,
superstition, rude and unwashed 'characters' and their offensive
shouts and mutterings. We have left all that behind.

And do not speak of God, or gods, or stones heaved up
for some strange, long-forgotten purpose. None of that mist
or mystery for us. It was mere ignorance, and we are done with it.
We have everything that we could wish for. What else is there
to have?

It's a Long Way

Gail Ross

It's a long way
From Home to Holyrood.

That year when the Parliament
Opened its doors
On a new session,
Elected people and local heroes,
Singers and Poets
And…Vikings,
The Garden Lobby rang
With ideas and hope,
The expectations of a new term.
And we laughed,

The totality of normality
Was zero,
But you liked it that way.
Routine is over rated,
But even spontaneity can get predictable.

Rules were laid out,
Some unwritten still,
Codes of conduct,
Newspaper columns, interviews,
Meetings and greetings,
The chamber
Vast and wooden,
The debut speech.

Committees, events, craic,
Legislation and policy,
Papers and papers and...
Papers.
It wasn't a long way to Margo's
Of an evening.

And you slink from the building
Like a Caithness cat
On the Caithness Flagstone,
Ready to do it all again
Next week.

Memorable events,
Supporting inclusive education,
Recognising local achievements,
And having THE most beautiful constituency,
No contest, no doubt.
The Beast from the East,
When Edinburgh was frozen and wild.
Could it be that the best irons are forged
When the fire is hottest?
It was cold that night,
But sometimes magic is made
When times are toughest.

You know some will stay,
Some will go,
Fitting in can be challenging,
Toleration is sometimes
All you can ask for,
All you can give.

It is a long way,
A road, a rail, a sky trail,
Journeys are made as
Easily as friends,
As diverse as the people
Represented,
And as crucial
As the causes championed,
As fraught as an
Opposition debate,
And welcome like the voting bell
After an eight hour
Stage three.

Couldn't you jump on a train?
A common refrain,
Education required often
On Highland geography,
No, Inverness is not nearly home

The honour of a lifetime,
A once in a generation
Opportunity,
The expectation on shoulders
That creak under its weight,
And yet the judge and the jury
Rumbles and grumbles,
But still the sun shines
On memories
That will never fade.

As the door clicks shut
For the final time
On a reluctant achievement,
Small arms open
With love.

It's a long way
From Holyrood to Home
Five years, to be precise.

His Mouth Full of Dying Fires

Finola Scott

On the simmer-dim shore
ocean meets time, whispers.
A moon-bright heron hauls dark,
loose-weaves the islands.
Loam, rock, tang and wear.

I'm harboured here for the music
but ghosts tangle at every corner.
Magnus, hearth-makers, Margaret Tait,
long-booted whaler men, Maxwell Davis
all go gently, leave soft shadows.

Head bowed with memory
heart full of legend,
bones shaped by history,
he's sure footed as a corncrake.
arms cradling craft.

A tweed figure hunches up a wynd
a pub falls open, pals welcome.
The wind catches words, rhythms.
His face weather-worn, sculpted
by tales and silence.

Notes
The title of the poem is taking from George Mackay Brown's 'Hamnavoe Market'.

Madras Morning

After 'Hamnavoe' – a humble offering

Leela Soma

Orangey mustard streaks the lightening sky
the cool morning sun spreads rays of gold
the soft dew weeps on the flowering white buds
blades of grass sway to the morning breeze.

The Gurkha opens the gate stretching his sleepy arms
ayah sweeps the veranda, bent over her broom
cook roasts the coffee beans delicious aroma rises
the milk boils as he turns the handle of the grinder.

The flicked radio sings the *'Suprapadam'*,
the dawn raga lifts the soul as the Lord is awakened.
Quiet meditation, the start of a lovely dawn
broken, piece by piece as day breaks.

Sonnet

For GMB

Ian Spring

For centuries the horseman's furrows stitched
this tapestry of land; waves knotting washed
to sand tokens of lives lived here and there,
echoes of the sea-kissed songs of sailors lost.

Time ran, and the fields raged with seed and the
supplicant fish were landed. Chancel, choir,
sanctuary were wrought from famous words and
nests of stones that could not breach or wither.

And the ploughboy mouthed words and blithely walked
with his lass; light as leaf in the high sun
of summer. And the crofters, fishwives, drunks
with dry mouths wished the dusk and their day done.

All for a soft silent boy, with sad eyes
reaping stories from stones and toil and salt soil.

Selkies, and my Sorrow

Courtney Stoddart

selkies and sorrow seep past me
and I too, shed my skin
I weep
for my courage creeps beneath me
I have a voice
but to raise her from her grave
is deadly
necromancy is a sin
but so is not to answer a calling
when it knocks upon your door
come rain, high hills or valley storms

ignore your truth
and become body of lies
become deceit
become the enemy
you thought you should defeat
battle not with fury
for it comes at a cost
and battle not with arrogance
or humility becomes your loss
and listen not just with ears
but with your whole being
and cast not wicked eyes
upon the living and the breathing
jealousy and envy eat up warm insides
and that cold and beastly storm

connives inside your pride

and seep not into darkness

lest the darkness creeps in you

watch the crying skies bleed

from black to blue

wrestles not with stars, with bark nor leaves

let compassion embrace your heart

as the oceans hold the seas

For George Mackay Brown

Sheila Templeton

Ye hinna gin awa, ye're aye here
in that mixter-maxter o saut watter
an yird, whaur creel mells wi ploo,
shore-fowk wi shepherds,
the siller o fish an the gowd o corn.

Ye glint in ilka wave landin starnies
in the dairk o the voe; in the meen's wame
as she githers ilka tide; in aa the glisterin
slabs o peat cut fae *the black chaos
o fire at the earth's centre.*

Yer vyce rasps yet in the crunch o a hamebound
keel; soughs skinklin beards o barley – is there
in ivery laach liftin the roof aff a winter howff,
gweed bleeze cheerin and gless brimmin ower.

Ye niver left.

George Mackay Brown X Gerard Manley Hopkins

Samuel Tongue

The old go, one by one, like guttered flames.
What's heaven? A sea chest with a thousand gold coins.
Carve the runes. Then be content with silence
for the three agonies – love, birth, death.

What's heaven? A sea chest with a thousand gold coins
and all is seared with trade; bleared, smeared with toil
and the three agonies: love, birth, death.
Each mortal thing does one thing and the same,

is seared with trade; bleared, smeared with toil.
A set of cups, a calendar, some chairs –
each mortal thing does one thing and the same.
The cupboard will have its loaf and bottle, come winter.

A set of cups, a calendar, some chairs
and man's mounting spirit in his bone-house:
the cupboard will have its loaf and bottle. Come winter,
it will flame out, like shining from shook foil

in man's mounting spirit. Into this bone-house,
the old go, one by one, like guttered flames,
and flame out like shining from shook foil.
Now carve the runes. Be content with silence.

Orkney Storms

In memory of George Mackay Brown

_____

Lynn Valentine

Shillins o rain coin thi hoose in noise
       coos sweeten their bit o dry
           wi muscle an mulk.

      Thi masked heids o Hoy wear gray.

      A scriever's banes waatch at Warbeth,
      gows snatch his poems fae thi air.

Hamnavoe shuttered, knees drawn
       tae hairths an fauchled dugs.

Luve's impermanence waits fir us
       scrievit oan risin tides.

Pilgrimage

Lynn Valentine

here is the seat outside the museum
here spars of oak, washed by sea
here a thief eagle rising
here are the hills more grey than green
mimicking your jaw-line
here is the honey
here the blue plaque
here yards of daffodils
and roses

Blackening

Stephen Watt

Just remember, this is a show of local love.
To be captured, kidnapped, snatched
in broad daylight. Fastened
to the rear of an open back pickup truck.

Cables are fettered round ankles.
Hands are taped behind post.
It begins gently
with propelled porridge oats

       then flour is showered
over saturated heads. Infinite buckets
of expired alcohol
and sawdust employed to absorb the mess.
People hurl vegetable peel, dog food,
feathers, raw duck eggs,
mayonnaise, fish, a year's supply
of dead daddy-long-legs

but it's because we love you.

This black *goo* will ward off evil spirits.
I promise – and so do all your relatives.
Pinned against a fence
or rolled down a hill,
you will lose shoes, trousers, your mind
to the sound of pots and pans
banging like tribal drums.

But at the bottom,
where you shed your clothes,
a high-pressure power hose
                    e r u p t s
like familiar Gaelic folk songs in a pub
and we will toast you and your immortal love
until the days
that become as blackened as this.

One Writer's Day, Early 2021

With apologies to George Mackay Brown

Jay Whittaker

WAKING
Frost on the attic window.
    Wrestle the dog into her coat.
    Counting down the minutes
        to the paid-for hours.

CLOCKED
Username, password. Return.
    Clack of keyboard. Back-to-back meetings.
    Our pixelated selves armoured, shabby kitchens hidden,
        by generic corporate backdrops.

TEATIME SAUNTER
My usual route to Craighouse fenced off
    - asbestos revealed after landslip –
    past luxury flats, the converted asylum.
        Trace a new path.

LONG VIEW
This triangulation point didn't used to be busy:
    folk on blankets picnic, gazing over roofs, spires,
    the turquoise Forth, to Fife, all the hills
        out of our reach, not yet permitted.

AND YET

I cast a poet to my TV from 300 miles away,
  her reading streams to every room.
   I potter, make cheese on toast, pour red wine.
    In online chat, I praise her closing lines.

SILENCE

Draw the blind against LED streetlight,
  light a candle, lean into shadow.
  The timer clicks off the lamp.
   Keep writing.

Draan Trow

Christie Williamson

aathin cheenged
eftir dy bluid
sweet needle

haaled aa da wandrin
worset o da universe
intae shaep

da lens widenin
laek a fat net
dodgin da Yesnaby crush

een glindrin
trow da bonded
gowld licht

ta see da best
in show
an aa da rest

wis choost da wye
it aye hed bön

wis choost da wye
du saa an sed

Making a Homeland

For Jacqueline

Neil Young

A sick and ageing Labrador in the car's back seat,
boot stuffed with clothes and £65 to our name,
at least we've got giros to claim
and your pal's empty house to use as our own,
spare time to write best-sellers
after I flicked a V to another take-the-piss boss
with his largesse of *extending your short-term contract*.
Not much to show at forty-five for a supposed career
but maverick honour exacts a price
and here in the layby I'm glad we've taken the shot:
The car, at least, is paid for and, hey, open-top –
the spoils of a well-paid job in your previous life –
and there is this sign saying
Welcome to Scotland/Failte Gu Alba
and for a while as we inhale crisp April air
infused with wet grass and heather
we're magnetised by something new,
expelling residual strains of what we've left,
those cold migrations of the past:
childhood ferry journeys, evictions,
demos, pickets and Maggie's millions,
checkpoints and the dole. We're scattered:
that's our inheritance. So strange
to our roots that our names could be accidents,
now lugging our pans by Vorschprungdonkey,

feeling rich for a day on last month's pay.
I say I'm tired of being bounced from city to town,
chasing dead-end jobs, not knowing where
or for how I'll belong. You give me a look;
and in those minutes we seal the unwritten pact
that will sustain us: this is our Rubicon;
foot to the floorboard and no going back
by anyone's curse or demand.
Though we might be from everywhere else,
we're of that mongrel band who make/remake
our kith and clan. And we will do that in this land.

GEORGE MACKAY BROWN BY ALASDAIR GRAY

(COURTESY OF *SPECTRUM* MAGAZINE)

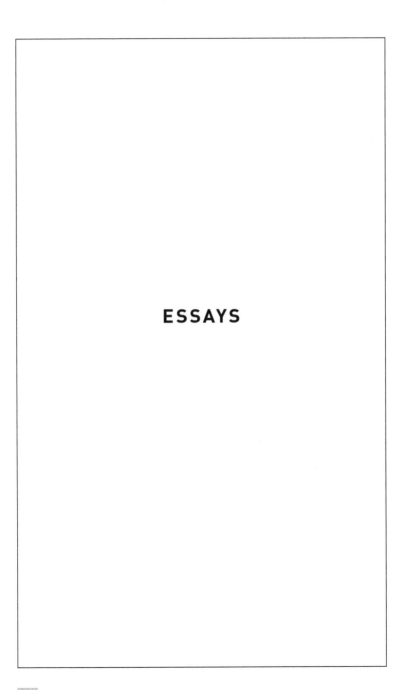

ESSAYS

Weaving the Threads

Pamela Beasant

An Orkney Tapestry sits quietly at the heart of George Mackay Brown's prolific output as a writer of poetry, stories, novels and plays, created over a lifetime that was longer and richer than he or anyone else expected. (Following a diagnosis of TB as a young man, before the introduction of penicillin, he must have felt he was living on borrowed time for almost all his adult life.) For those who have never read him, this small book about his native Orkney serves as a wonderful introduction. For those who have already fallen under his spell, it is something they return to and quote from, and love like an old friend.

My copy is tatty, well-thumbed and browning, and full of torn strips of paper marking certain passages. With its drawings by GMB's friend, the Orkney artist Sylvia Wishart, the book has an evocative magic; just to hold it conjures up George and his Orkney, more than anything else he wrote. Somehow, Orkney and George are fused, and while Stromness, his home town, seems to have absorbed him in its stone walls, piers and crow steps, his absence is still noticeable, a gap in the town, which has changed over the years but also stayed essentially the same. In 2021, it will be 100 years since he was born and 25 years since he died, but I still miss him. (My first ten years in Stromness overlapped with George's last, during which we had a quiet but strong bond to do with poetry, shy on my part.) Picking up *An Orkney Tapestry* is like hearing his voice again.

It's a hard book to sum up because it's a bit of a mishmash of history, description, essay, poetry and even a short play. It shouldn't hold together at all, but it does, wonderfully, and in fact the pure essence of GMB as a writer is here, set down in his characteristically distilled, poetic prose. The book started out as a commission, and the assumption is that the publishers had in mind a kind of contemporary guidebook to the islands as seen through his eyes. But that kind of writing, involving facts, figures, lists and much tedious research, was not to his taste, and he turned the commission into an opportunity to encapsulate all that was precious and rich about the land and the people of Orkney, in the face of dubious progress, the pernicious influence of television, and the uniformity of thought and opinion imposed by the mass media.

For GMB, everything had a context or a ghost: words, thoughts, stories and people; and everyone in the islands was woven together with a shared history and 'fable' (or vision) of themselves, based on the past, which is everywhere evident in the islands. He wanted Orkney people to understand and be proud of this fable, and to define their uniqueness in the context of a kind of woven garment of history.

GMB was born in 1921, and he wrote *An Orkney Tapestry* in his late forties when, after a long, slow start, he was truly finding his voice as a writer and his place as a fully-fledged and independent person. At the time of writing his mother had recently died and he had moved into his own council flat in Stromness. He had emerged from some years of heavy drinking verging on alcoholism; he was gaining recognition as a poet and short-story writer and he was firmly back in his home town after his only spell away from Orkney at Newbattle Abbey College and Edinburgh University.

Not only that: after the failure of his brief engagement to Stella Cartwright, the 'muse' of many of the Edinburgh poets, he was accepting (not unhappily) that he was destined to remain single, live alone and dedicate himself to writing. Also, significantly, he had converted to Catholicism, rejecting his Presbyterian upbringing; a bold and unusual step in Orkney. He had found himself, and his voice, and in some ways *An Orkney Tapestry* is his manifesto as a writer, and all his creative and spiritual preoccupations and inspirations can be found in this book: the Sagas, the lives of St Magnus and St Rognvald, the Christ figure, the ordinary people, the land, the sea, the drunks and outsiders, and the communities which are sources of strength, resilience and continuity, as well as judgement and narrow-mindedness.

Apart from anything else, the book also contains his most captivating description of the Orkney landscape and weather:

> A city shower is a meaningless nuisance, a liquidity seeping into collar and trouser-leg. In the north, on a showery day, you can see the rain, its lovely behaviour over an island – while you stand a mile off in a patch of sun – Jock's cows in the meadow a huddle of ghosts, Tammy's oat field jewelled; the clouds a rout of fabulous creatures dissolving at last through their prism... Nothing is more lovely than the islands in a shifting dapple of sun and rain.

This section is simply a beautiful piece of prose – a master-class in succinct and balanced sentences. And his celebration of January's 'star-hung skies' is touching, coming from someone who dreaded the illness the long dark days might bring.

There's a whole chapter on Rackwick, in North Hoy, one of the most beautiful and rarefied places in Orkney, which GMB loved and often visited. For him, the beauty of the place was underscored by the harshness of the lives of the people who had eked a meagre living from the land and dangerous sea. The valley was gradually depopulated until the only farmer left there, Jack Rendall, married, and the first child born in Rackwick for many years, Lucy, arrived in 1980 – a joyful, hopeful event, celebrated in GMB's acrostic poem 'Lullaby for Lucy', and later set to music by Peter Maxwell Davies.

Published in 1969, *An Orkney Tapestry* was still fresh and new when Peter Maxwell Davies (Max) came on holiday to Orkney in 1970. He bought the book in Stromness, stayed up all night reading it and, by one of those strange coincidences, met George the following day in Hoy and first set eyes on Bunertoon, a ruined cottage high up on the cliff at Rackwick, which would become his home for the next 30 years. GMB's poetry inspired some beautiful new music, not least the opera *The Martyrdom of St Magnus*, which opened the first St Magnus Festival in 1977. From that chance meeting, based on Max's enthusiasm for *An Orkney Tapestry*, so much grew.

And yet, *An Orkney Tapestry* remains out of print, at GMB's own request. It's to be found fairly easily second-hand, but it's an intriguing and troubling thought that GMB himself was not happy with the book. He was characteristically tight-lipped about the reasons for this. Perhaps he felt it was a bit of a jumble of thoughts and ideas. Perhaps the very things that people love about it did not please him (he was a severe self-critic). It was certainly longer than anything he had written before, and his under-confidence about his ability to sustain a long piece of prose, expressed when his publisher suggested a novel, might be based on a sense of failure to make a coherent whole of *An Orkney Tapestry*. And yet, very soon after, he went on to write the wonderful *Greenvoe*, followed by a string of others, culminating in *Beside the Ocean of Time*, shortlisted for the Booker Prize in 1994.

For me, everything GMB wrote came from a deep well of poetry, and a poet's sensibility informs the beauty and distillation of his prose. He is sometimes portrayed as a diffident, even naïve writer, which might be true in some sense, but he knew what he was trying to achieve, and he knew he was good. Far from being some sort of 'mystic sage', he was funny, occasionally mischievous and very interested in the doings of the town. He worked with great discipline through illness and bouts of depression, and was a generous, perceptive mentor to younger writers.

From his flat in Stromness, he roved through time and space, and channelled his single-minded vision into a body of work that speaks universally. And in the lovely conglomeration of *An Orkney Tapestry* he wove a portrait, a fable for Orkney, whose ongoing threads are deeply rooted here in the islands, but encompass everyone.

'Rhythms and Images and Legends are Everywhere': George Mackay Brown's Orkney

Linden Bicket

In an essay for *Chapman* magazine written in 1976, George Mackay Brown reflected on his early influences, literary craft and poetic preoccupations. In this short piece, he recognised that Orkney was the centre of all he wrote and noted that he was fortunate to have been raised on the islands, because 'There could be no better setting for an artist'. Brown admitted: 'I don't need to go in search of themes. Rhythms and images and legends are everywhere. To utter a name or a word is to set the whole web trembling'.[1]

One hundred years on from George Mackay Brown's birth, Orkney remains the beating heart of his poetry, prose and drama. Brown's poetry brings together Orcadian folklore and myth, the agricultural wheel of the year, and the history of Orkney's people and communities. His poetic universe is shaped by a distinctly Scottish, Catholic spirituality, and this underpins all his collections, from *The Storm* (1954) to his posthumously published *Travellers* (2001). This essay will explore the richly delicate web of Orkney as Brown imagined it over several decades in his poetry.

The poem 'Themes' from *Loaves and Fishes* (1959) helpfully distils some of Brown's major concerns as a poet into a short, melodic list. 'Love and birth' are mentioned alongside

---

1   George Mackay Brown, 'Writer's Shop', *Chapman* [1976], pp.100-1 (2002), pp.249-52 (250-1).

'Odyssean corn' which rejuvenates barren 'furrows of death'.[2] The poem ends with an evocative couplet which declares that the key players in Brown's literary Orkney are 'Women scanning the sea; Ploughmen wounding the earth'.[3] However, the first of these categories – 'love and birth' – is somewhat neglected in criticism of Brown's work. He is without doubt a poet of childhood, and his poetry meditates on his own boyhood, as well as celebrating and marking the birth of new generations of Orcadians.

In *Following a Lark* (1996), published just after Brown's death, there is, writes Maggie Fergusson, 'a powerful nostalgia for infancy'.[4] The poem which introduces this collection, 'Following a Lark: A Country Boy Goes to School', contrasts the freedom of childhood outdoors with the sterility and boredom of the classroom. The child speaker of the poem sits at his desk and thinks, dreamily, 'I wish I was that tinker boy / Going on over the hill, the wind in his rags'.[5] Freedom and nonconformity are embodied by the Traveller (or 'tinker') frequently in Brown's work. Ragged, ambiguous figures, Brown's Travellers are on the margins of polite society, they retain a link to pre-Reformation Scotland (through a residual Catholicism) and are unconstrained by convention and societal obligation.

Brown brings this idea to life most fully in his short story 'Five Green Waves' (*A Calendar of Love*, 1967), in which a young male protagonist truants from school and encounters Sarah, a

---

2 George Mackay Brown, 'Themes' in Archie Bevan and Brian Murray (eds), *The Collected Poems of George Mackay Brown* (2005), p.21, l. 4, l. 5, l. 6.

3 'Themes', ll.7-8.

4 Maggie Fergusson, *George Mackay Brown: The Life* (2006), p.285.

5 George Mackay Brown, 'Following a Lark: A Country Boy Goes to School' in *Collected Poems*, pp.317-19, ll.30-1.

Traveller girl, on the beach. Like the speaker of Brown's poem, the boy of 'Five Green Waves' longs to escape the requirements imposed on him by school and polite social mores. He finds that Sarah's hair 'smelt of ditch-water and grass fires', and 'her red dress fell open at the shoulder where the button had come out of it'.[6] She embodies all the unconventionality and romance that the unnamed boy longs for as he wanders the island shoreline. In this short story, the bust of Shelley 'with wild blank eyes' signals that the liberty and radicalism of Romanticism have been crushed and neutralised by a restrictive system of education.[7] Meanwhile, in 'A Country Boy Goes to School' a fragment of Wordsworth's 'I Wandered Lonely as a Cloud'[8] nods to Brown's schoolboy experience of learning poetry dutifully by rote in what he called 'the dark prison of school'.[9] It is striking how consistently this poem from Brown's final collection mirrors 'Five Green Waves' – a short story from his first volume of short fiction. Brown has sometimes been criticised for being repetitive, but this mirroring signals that his themes and ideas matured and evolved across decades. His later work is in powerful dialogue with his earliest ideas and shows that the wholeness of his poetic vision was something that remained consistent throughout his entire career.

---

6 George Mackay Brown, 'Five Green Waves' in *A Calendar of Love* [1967] (1970), pp.51, 50.

7 'Five Green Waves', p.42.

8 'A Country Boy Goes to School', l. 46.

9 'Writer's Shop', p249. Brown recalled: 'The way we were taught in school in those days to appreciate poetry was enough to put anybody off. We had to learn by rote a stanza every week and then stand up one after the other and utter the meaningless jargon'. However, he quotes Wordsworth's 'Fidelity' as an example of 'a stanza [that] would open like an oasis in the desert'. 'Writer's Shop', p.250.

As well as being a poet of childhood, Brown is also a chronicler of the richly elemental world of sea, earth, seasons, patterns and cycles, and it is absolutely true that eternally recurring 'Odyssean corn' is an image and symbol which can be traced throughout his poetry and prose. 'Countryman' – first published in the collection *Voyages* (1983) – condenses the life of an Orcadian down to seven couplets replete with agricultural metaphor. This poem reflects again on the key theme of 'birth and love', as Brown's countryman begins life as 'a swaddled wail', who dutifully goes 'with jotter and book and pencil to school'.[10] After marriage vows 'To the long white sweetness under blessing and bell', come children and old age.[11] Here, as elsewhere in Brown's work, the poet uses agricultural analogy to express something of human life in its connection to the divine. In having a family and producing children, the country-man and his wife reap 'a full harvest, / Utterings of gold at the mill'.[12] But this is no simple pastoral metaphor; nor is it a sign of what Douglas Gifford deems Brown's 'almost pagan view of Orkney'.[13] The harvesting of corn is seen sacramentally in all Brown's work. A Catholic convert, he recognised and returned continually to the Eucharistic symbolism that he found in Orkney's harvests.[14] While Christopher Whyte, like Gifford, finds that 'his weaving of agricultural process and the narrative of the crucifixion is, of course, heterodox', Brown's writing delights in his Orcadian book of nature, which reveals a creator God and provides a storehouse of images that describe and

10 George Mackay Brown, 'Countryman' in *Collected Poems*, p.222, l.2, l.4.

11 'Countryman', l.8.

12 'Countryman', ll.9–10.

13 Douglas Gifford, Sarah Dunnigan and Alan MacGillivray (eds), *Scottish Literature* (2002), p.840.

14 For more on critical readings of heterodoxy and paganism in Brown's work, see Linden Bicket, *George Mackay Brown and the Scottish Catholic Imagination* (2017).

chart the life cycle of every individual.[15]

Indeed, Brown's depictions of the natural world ally him with a canon of Catholic authors and poets (including Gerard Manley Hopkins, the subject of Brown's unfinished doctoral research) who find the sacred in the ordinary. Brown noted:

> I try often to suggest the swift dangerous rhythms of the sea, and (even more important) the slow dark fruitful rhythm of the earth from seedtime to harvest. [...] The bread that is the result of the crofter's hard labour on the earth is a recurring symbol: meaning the simple nourishment of the body, and the mysterious sign of the godhead.[16]

In 'Countryman', Brown exploits this symbolism fully. While children are a 'full harvest' in the poem, by the end of the countryman's life, he is characterised by 'old yarns, old malt, near the hearthstone'.[17] Like the harvest, the countryman's life has ripened and, after many years (or stages of distillation) it is likened to a rich malt whisky.

In fact, the preciousness and transience of life is a topic that Brown returned to very often in his poetic corpus. 'Bird in the Lighted Hall' (also published in *Voyages*, 1983) uses a parable borrowed from the Venerable Bede – that of 'the life of man on earth' as 'the swift flight of a single sparrow through [a] banqueting hall'.[18] In Brown's poem, a bard explains:

---

15 Christopher Whyte, *Modern Scottish Poetry* (2004), p.170.

16 George Mackay Brown, *The Orcadian Poet George Mackay Brown Reads His Poems and a Story* [LP sleeve notes] (1971).

17 'Countryman', p.222, ll.11-12.

18 D H Farmer (ed) and Leo Sherley-Price (trans), *Bede, Ecclesiastical History of the English People*, (1990), p.129.

Bright door, black door,
Beak-and-wing hurtling through,
This is life.
(Childhood lucent as dew,
The opening rose of love,
Labour at plough and oar,
The yellow leaf,
The last blank of snow.)[19]

Life is a ritual cycle of birth, childhood, love, toil and death, and the archetypal simplicity of this perspective is expressed by Brown's economic language and haiku-like verse form. He noted frequently that his writing was informed by the starkness of the Icelandic sagas, writing: 'I try to use brevity and silence [...] to reveal more than lavish description and dialogue can'.[20] Here, form, language and subject matter converge to produce a brief but evocative meditation on the life of Orkney's people and communities across centuries. And although his impact on Brown is sometimes exaggerated in in appraisals of their work,[21] his early teacher Edwin Muir's writings on 'the story and the fable' – or the connection between the life of man and the broader fable of humankind – is a clear textual undercurrent here, albeit one baptised by the intertextual connection with Bede.

Brown's identification of 'labour at plough and oar' in 'Bird in the Lighted Hall' also highlights his recurrent pairing of sea and land, or fishermen with ploughs (the title of his fifth volume of poetry in 1971). His poetry and prose are populated by hard-drinking, stoical crofters and fisherman, as well as

---

19 George Mackay Brown, 'Bird in the Lighted Hall' in *Collected Poems*, pp.201-2, ll.1-9.

20 *The Orcadian Poet*.

21 See *George Mackay Brown and the Scottish Catholic Imagination*, p.66.

male storytellers, monks and Vikings, making his literary universe an unarguably masculine one. In the character study 'Halcro' (from *Loaves and Fishes*, 1959), the poem's speaker warns against engaging the titular character in pleasantries and polite conversation. Brown's ageing Halcro wants 'salty texts' – news of 'how the corn's ripening', as well as reports of bar fights and beautiful women.[22] Impart this news, the speaker says, and

> Then see his bone-bright hands
> Frail on the chair, grow firm again
> In the stillness of old brawls,
> Torn nets, sweet dust, and tangled grain.[23]

Halcro's masculinity is defined by his work wrenching a living from the reluctant sea and stubborn soil. His 'torn nets' and 'tangled grain' indicate a life of toughness and endurance on sea and land and reinforce a machismo that is leavened only by the smallest hint of sweetness, or femininity. In this way, Halcro is an Orcadian successor of the Vikings, who (in common with many of Brown's male creations), owes much to codes of masculinity in works by writers like Ernest Hemingway. Indeed, Brown regarded Hemingway's terse style as being 'closest to the spirit' of the Icelandic sagas.[24] Halcro is also a literary descendant of Captain Cat of Dylan Thomas's *Under Milk Wood* (1954), who dreams of his days at sea and tells his ghostly lover, Rosie Probert, 'Lie down, lie easy. Let me shipwreck in your thighs'.[25] Thomas's pairing of sex and death is one eagerly taken up by his admirer Brown in poems like 'Old Fisherman with Guitar' (*The Year of the Whale*, 1965), in

22 George Mackay Brown, 'Halcro' in *Collected Poems*, p.27, l.11.
23 'Halcro', ll.21-4.
24 George Mackay Brown, *For the Islands I Sing* (1997), p.65.
25 Dylan Thomas, *Under Milk Wood* in *Dylan Thomas Omnibus* [1995] (2014), p.376.

which we are told that the fisherman's hands have, in his youth, cut 'The strong / Crab-eaten corpse Jock washed from a boat' and 'gathered the mouth of Thora to his / mouth'.[26]

Clearly, Brown's theme of 'ploughmen wounding the earth' is, as he suggested, an important part of his corpus, but what of 'women scanning the sea'? Critics have been swift to diagnose female passivity in Brown's writing and Brown admitted that in his work 'the tendency always is to associate men with what is dangerous, exploratory, breaking open and casting down, and women with endless waiting, patience, consolation'.[27] In his analysis of 'Gudrun' (from *Fishermen with Ploughs*, 1971), Whyte rightly notes that 'the image of woman as jar, as vessel, pervades the entire poem', and he argues that 'here, as else-where in Mackay Brown's work, woman's role as receptacle is so emphasised as to overshadow other possible roles and functions'.[28] It is impossible to deny that women are allied very often with reproduction in Brown's work. His writing is populated by wives, mothers and women whose role seems to be mainly to produce children. Perhaps the best example of this is Alice Voar, the dreamy young mother of seven in Brown's first novel, *Greenvoe* (1972), whose 'uninhibited sensuality' is without question her key characteristic.[29] Brown writes: 'Deep within her Alice nourished the root of love. Alice cherished it with all the slumberous warmth of her body. Alice curled languorously about the exotic seed'.[30] However inescapable these sensual and domestic characterisations, there are also

---

26 George Mackay Brown, 'Old Fisherman with Guitar' in *Collected Poems*, pp.46-7, ll.10-11, ll.12-13.

27 *For the Islands I Sing*, p.178.

28 *Modern Scottish Poetry*, pp.169-70.

29 Alan Bold, *George Mackay Brown* (1978), p.91.

30 George Mackay Brown, *Greenvoe* (1972), p.235.

women of deep complexity in Brown's work. The titular character of 'Celia' (*A Time to Keep*, 1969), with her despairing theological questions, the princess of *Time in a Red Coat* (1984) whose purpose is to slay the dragon of war, and the spirited Sophie of *Beside of the Ocean of Time* (1994) are all multifaceted creations whose relationship with place, time and history is interrogated within Brown's fictional universe.

Women also play a central role in Brown's depiction of faith and the ecclesiastical history of Orkney. A central figure in Brown's corpus (and one who has received a good deal of critical attention elsewhere) is Orkney's patron saint, Magnus.[31] Alongside works exploring his life and martyrdom, Brown wrote a number of poems dedicated to female saints. One of the shortest and most luminous of these is 'Lighting Candles in Midwinter' (from *Voyages*, 1983):

> Saint Lucy, see
> Seven bright leaves in the winter tree
>
> Seven diamonds shine
> In the deepest darkest mine
>
> Seven fish go, a glimmering shoal
> Under the ice of the North Pole
>
> Sweet St Lucy, be kind
> To us poor and wintered and blind.[32]

The fourth-century virgin martyr Lucy is commemorated in this brief poem of four couplets. Here, in keeping with tradition and with the saint's iconography, Brown riffs on Lucy's

---

31 See Bicket, pp.111-41.

32 George Mackay Brown, 'Lighting Candles in Midwinter' in *Collected Poems*, p.214.

associations with light. Lucy, whose eyes were put out before she was killed, is venerated on her feast day of thirteenth December and is patron saint of the blind. In this poem she illuminates the gloom of a long Orcadian winter, shedding kindly light on trees, the earth, the sea and humanity, who all search the winter darkness for comfort and consolation. Brown makes sure to repeat the number seven ('a mysterious and beautiful number') throughout, signalling his lifelong interest in exploring pattern, harmony and ritual within his verse.[33]

Ultimately, Brown's vision of Orkney's rich treasury of community, history and lore as a 'web' has much to tell us about his holistic view of his Orcadian milieu. In Brown's Orkney, all life is a richly connected and inter-reliant ecosystem. The elements yield sustenance for body and soul. The seasons turn liturgically, a constant reminder of the hand of the divine in ordinary matter. Stories, passed down by generations, nourish the imagination. Brown once mentioned casually (and possibly with sly humour) that he hoped his work would be remembered 'maybe seven or eight generations hence'.[34] And while the poem ('A Work for Poets') that is quoted on his gravestone instructs 'Carve the runes / Then be content with silence', it is likely that the works of this chronicler of Orkney will linger in the consciousness for as long, or even longer, than he once hoped.[35]

---

33 *For the Islands I Sing*, p.68.

34 Lucy Lethbridge, 'Orkney Boy', *New Statesman*, 27 March 2006.

35 George Mackay Brown, 'A Work for Poets' in *Collected Poems*, p.378, ll.13-14.

The Everyday and the Eternal

Erin Farley

Every Thursday for more than twenty-five years, beginning in 1971 and continuing until his death in 1996, George Mackay Brown sent a 'Letter from Hamnavoe' to the assembled readers of *The Orcadian* newspaper. These columns reflect on life in contemporary Stromness and open a warmly lit window into Brown's thoughts, inspirations, and daily routines. The letters are only around four hundred words long, but each is very much itself. Three book-length collections of the columns have been published, as *Letters from Hamnavoe* (first published in 1975), *Under Brinkie's Brae* (1979) and *Rockpools and Daffodils* (1992).

In the 'Letter from Hamnavoe', Brown speaks to the reader as if they had dropped in for a visit or come across the author enjoying the sunshine outside his door. Sometimes they recount an episode from Orkney history or a childhood memory. They might comment on the latest development proposals in Stromness, or on a book he had recently enjoyed (or, as in one of my favourites, the dangers of leaving the end of a bottle of strawberryade too close to the soup pot on a winter's evening).[1] They are the stuff of the everyday, a kind of nature writing in their charting of the light and weather of the Orkney year, and a kind of prose poetry in the vivid imagery distilled into their few paragraphs.

Newspapers are, by definition, impermanent. Unlike the sacred object of the book, no one bats an eyelid if, reading completed, you line the bin with them or stuff them into wet

---

1 'Strawberry Flavoured Ham Broth' (1 February 1979), George Mackay Brown, *Under Brinkie's Brae* (2003), p.189.

shoes. Brown himself, in a column on daily newspapers – not to be confused with the weekly in which these words appeared – admitted he could live without them: 'I'd rather be reading a good book than stuffing myself with wads of newsprint, night after night. But a pile of newspapers comes in handy, right enough. When you're setting the fire, for example'.[2] The weekly newspaper has a slightly longer lifespan, but in the cosmic scheme of time, not by much. Brown would often write next week's column on a Thursday morning, *Orcadian* publication day, at the same time that the one he'd written the week before was making its way into the world. They didn't need to last any longer than that. They could live their seven days, and no one could ask any more of them. But the ephemeral is quietly tenacious, and it builds a web of meaning around us.

The local newspaper is a particular kind of print space, a hubbub of voices translated into ink and paper geography. It is at heart a shared and often spoken text, traditionally home not only to 'hard news' but also to a whole host of stories, poems and snippets to be read aloud and passed along. Like the community it represents, the newspaper arranges itself around a set of shared landmarks. The most dramatic is often the letters page, a town square where views are exchanged gently or furiously. By its side comes the busy marketplace bartering of classified adverts, the notices of coming events. The ritual centre of the newspaper, permanent yet ever-changing, is the birth, marriage and death notices.

It is easy to joke now about the reading of these as an old-fashioned habit or even a morbid compulsion – *wha's deid noo*?

---

2 'Daily Newspapers' (17 November 1983) in George Mackay Brown, *Rockpools and Daffodils* (2017), p.116.

– but there is power in the quietly stated reminder of shared kinship they record. And, like the priest's words at wedding or funeral, the marking of these things in black and white in this record of shared lives has ritual power to make them real.

In the space between these landmarks, news and columnists and regular features set out the week. Whether the author has it in mind or not, their piece will be one in a chorus of other voices – a chorus orchestrated by the editor's hand, but still one with a vital connection to the life of the place. When the 'Letter from Hamnavoe' appeared on *The Orcadian*'s page of Stromness news, below 'obituaries, reports of whist drives, old folks' outings, etc', it formed part of a conversation with the Orkney community and its diaspora.[3] This was the audience whose approval Brown valued most as a writer, and he used the space to explore shared memories and a common tradition.

The rhythms of local journalism shaped Brown's writing life from the beginning. In 1939, it was in *The Orkney Herald* newspaper that his first published poem, 'The Hills of Hoy at Sunset', appeared.[4] A few years later when Brown was in his twenties, directionless and struggling to recover from tuberculosis, *The Herald* editor recognised a writer with an ear for place and community and engaged him to cover goings-on in Stromness. As a reporter, he was tasked with staying tuned to murmurs of news around the town. But in George Mackay Brown's hands, the brief was expanded, with or without editorial blessing. The Stromness report gradually became the column 'Islandman', a series of vivid pictures of Orkney life and landscape as seen by a young man determinedly

---

3 George Mackay Brown, *Letters from Hamnavoe*, (2002), p.7.

4 Maggie Fergusson, *George Mackay Brown: The Life* (2006), p.42.

rooted in tradition. As Brown developed his identity as a writer, he gave into moments of youthful anger, and ventured into Devil's advocacy on occasion.[5] But it was also as 'Islandman' that he first described how the beauty of Rackwick in Hoy 'struck him like a blow', beginning a deep and lifelong creative relationship with the valley.[6]

In 1971, when Brown began writing the weekly 'Letter from Hamnavoe', he stood on the same Stromness shore with a far more secure sense of his presence in place and time. He was by then a critically acclaimed literary light, but he had no intention of playing the part of celebrity author. The role he sought in Orkney was that of an older kind of bard, a storyteller in and of the community. His corner of *The Orcadian* became a sort of fireside in print, to which he could invite all comers to share a quiet thought. Although Brown was no longer even nominally a 'reporter' on the events of Stromness, in his columns he charted ebbs and flows of feeling and fortune, eddies of history and tradition swirling round to catch on the present.

Orkney has a particular way of invoking the past. Light changes dramatically around the circle of a year, day and night rising and falling like tides. And in the landscape the lives of people who have been carried through the same cycles of light reach out from fields and roadsides, as Neolithic tombs and Second World War pillboxes. The compass points of equinoxes and solstices were deeply important to Brown. He observed them, both as nature and as sacred occasion. The days are marked in his columns as a time when people's connection to the world and to one another is illuminated in sunlight or candle flame,

5 *The Life*, p.74. Fergusson also notes that Brown later said he was uncomfortable with his youthful ability to 'sneer at people in print' in these early columns.

6 *The Life*, p.69.

'an interweaving, a poise, a dapple'.[7]

This builds a sense of time and history which is different to the linear one we have learned to work from. I think of it as a storyteller's sense of time, in which nothing is ever quite over, and you can feel the shape of the emerging future – if not its every detail – as the story unfolds. The Orkney storyteller Tom Muir once spoke to me about the sense that, every time you tell a story, you stand alongside everyone else who has ever told it, among a community called into being through the act of telling. Perhaps the people who will tell it in future gather too, in the shadows just ahead of us.

George Mackay Brown wrote with a storyteller's voice, with a clarity which defines his work in these columns and elsewhere. His writing says as much in as few words as a folktale. Brown could get closer to myth in writing than almost anyone else, reaching towards the pure verbal formula that will turn the wheel of the year and slay the dragon. In these columns, the voice of the bard weaves the daily life of twentieth-century Stromness, the small incidences and chance meetings shared by his community of readers, into that long tradition of sun and darkness and story. Brown does this even as he sometimes laments that 'newspapers spread a greyness' across the magic that once settled on the landscape.[8] But the local paper held space for these repeated meetings of poet and community in a way it is hard to imagine another form succeeding at.

In their embrace of the everyday and the eternal, George Mackay Brown's columns became a meeting place for myth and gossip, the twin threads of the oral tradition. Today, we

---

7 'Equinox' (28 September 1978) in *Under Brinkie's Brae*, p.171.

8 'Midsummer' (24 June 1976) in *Under Brinkie's Brae*, p.33.

often use 'gossip' to mean purely malicious talk, but it need not be so – the word's roots are in 'god-sib', the conversations between kin. I think of it here as a passing on of news, a sharing of life changes big and small to make them real, the brief exchanges in shops or street corners which remind us of wider connections. In the oral tradition, speech is both fleeting and eternal. Words last a moment, but their meaning settles into the space between people and builds kinship over years, and between generations.

George Mackay Brown's words were intended to endure. He spoke of an ambition for his writing to be remembered 'maybe seven or eight or nine generations hence'.[9] But equally he knew this could not be forced. All you can do is tell the story, and let it go to that place between worlds or seas or just between people, settling into the unspoken bonds of kinship: 'Carve the runes, then be content with silence'.[10] This repeated act of communi-cating, in speech or writing, is what makes us – as Brown put it – 'involved with mankind'.[11] And it is an involvement which traverses backwards and forwards in time. In their edited collections, the 'Letters from Hamnavoe' step back from the paper's busy town square of print. But in book form they are still arranged in year order, cycling round springs and winters.

And still, somehow, I can lift one of these books from the shelf and open it to a month thirty or forty years ago, and find it tells me something new and essential. On the Spring equinox in 2020, I came home from a workplace now closed to the public,

---

9   *The Life*, p.180.

10 This line, from his poem 'A Work For Poets', is inscribed on Brown's gravestone in Warbeth Cemetery.

11 George Mackay Brown, letter to Stella Cartwright, quoted in Ron Ferguson, *George Mackay Brown: The Wound and the Gift* (2011), p.315.

hands bitter with sanitiser, and opened *Rockpools and Daffodils*. I'd only bought it earlier that month, in the Orcadian Bookshop in Kirkwall during a visit to friends, and I hadn't yet read all of it. The pandemic began to truly set in while I was in Orkney, and I'd spent an eerie journey home watching news alerts pop up on my phone and trying not to breathe too much.

I leafed through the pages and looked for this point in the year. In late March 1988 (three months before I was born), Brown had written on 'Equinoctial Blues'. The levelling of light and darkness in late March often brought a 'leaden lump' of depression to his thoughts despite the promise of coming warmth. He spoke about the lang reed of hardship that this time of year once brought to Orkney, with winter stocks depleted and spring growth not yet sprung. It was clear by then that in 2020 we faced a long and unfamiliar reed. I was beginning to feel a despair that was echoed all around me, and none of us could pretend to have an answer to it. Brown, in Stromness decades before, was also facing a sense of hopelessness, haunted by the thought all human work would amount to 'a nothing' in the end. Nonetheless, he reflected:

> Of course, it doesn't amount to a nothing at all. We humans are so conditioned that we must always be doing or making something. Otherwise, we are obscurely convinced, chaos will come again. And so, in some way too subtle to be comprehended, every thought and every action sends delicate ripples through the whole web of creation, and influences not only the future but the past also...[12]

And we went onwards, into the growing light.

---

12 'Equinoctial Blues' (31 March 1988) in *Rockpools and Daffodils,* p.211.

Here Lies Betty Corrigall

Ingrid Leonard

> *Betty Corrigall lived on the island of Hoy, in Orkney, in the late 1770s. A woman in her late twenties, Betty, after becoming pregnant was abandoned by her love. The rebuke of her neighbours and the societal shame consigned to her led Betty to take her own life. As a suicide, she was buried outside the Kirk in an unmarked peat moor grave. Some 150 years later her coffin was rediscovered. In 1976 a headstone was provided to mark Betty's resting place; inscribed upon were the words, 'Here Lies Betty Corrigall'... George Mackay Brown took Betty as the subject of a poem and an essay, both simply entitled 'Betty Corrigall'.*

When they first found my coffin, they thought I might be treasure, for my grave is unmarked and I have no neighbours. Instead, peat and cotton stretch down to Scapa Flow and Gutter Sound, where I tried to make my home among bladder-wrack. I have lain on the boundary between Hoy and North Walls since the seventh decade of a forgotten century. I have islands in my view – Rysa, Fara and Cava – and shipwrecks lie round them in quiet menace.

One night, when I was new into my 27th year, I met a stranger at the dance with eyes the colour of cut peat and a smile hewn from an unfamiliar seam. My skirts swayed and our boots set in unison to the fiddler. The stranger's voice was the cream of butter fresh from the churn and we kissed in days that followed in stolen moments between chores, searching for lady's smock, dog violet. Wrapped in a blanket, we counted stars in the plough. The moon beamed upon hands rough and sweet, a trace of whisky on his breath. My insides were a new-kindled fire as I went about days, promises of betrothal ringing febrile in the curlew's call, the wobbly baa of lambs.

Until the days of sickness and my mother's watchful eye on the rag-pail. Words on islands are like sleet; they fall hard and fast and horizontal, into the damp air. He left before I had the chance to see him, my stranger, gone to sea on a murk-ridden day. What remained turned foul, curled inside me in dirt and disgust.

People around me turned dangerous: the threat of a blow when I went to fetch water, spit on my face as I walked. Talk of the day and its humours turned to whispers, prayers murmured against a poison that dripped ungodly in the midst of a people that kept to the ledger of seasons and laboured at abnegation. They looked at me and saw a woman who had tried to kill God, a reminder of life on a cliff's edge. Fear held me by throat and quim. My heart was a bank with a seam hawked through it.

I made for myself a green wool shawl but it didn't follow me. Instead, they put me in a hole with the rope I used to hang myself and no-one, not the kirk nor the lairds of Melsetter or Hoy, would suffer my body to lie on their land.

And so I demurred in coarse ground, godless and forgotten. Friends and neighbours set a seal over my transgression, their peace of mind bought with the dirty silver of superstition and the folk that give it a home, still belief comes with a price; my father howled in the night at Greengairs, heard the wind scream in wintertime and knew it as recrimination, sole companion for his lost girl tossed in a box. My mother's heart was quick to curdle.

The years passed and they found me again, my body unblemished in peat, dark hair curling around my shoulders, belly still soft. Soldiers digging me up in wonder until others sealed me in concrete.

Now I have a gravestone and a holy man whispers words over it. I am yards from the road and no homestead in sight. Some say there are more of us out here in the moss. Perhaps you will think of us when the wind howls, as we lie in the holes that were dug for us, sweet-faced and sorrowful, our heads in one land and our feet in another.

George Mackay Brown – A Biographical Note

Stuart MacBeath

It is said that George Mackay Brown, as he slipped out of consciousness in Balfour Hospital, Kirkwall, uttered one final line to the nurses who surrounded him. Typically, it was a statement powered by both his imagination and his lived experience: 'I see hundreds and hundreds of ships sailing out of the harbour'. Shortly afterwards, on 13 April 1996, Brown passed away at age 75 following a short illness. Death had lingered at the periphery of Brown's life since his diagnosis of tuberculosis in his late teens, yet in quiet resilience, he far outlived his initial prognosis.

Brown was born on 17 October 1921. The youngest of John Brown and Mhairi Mackay's six children, he was brought up in the place he would remain for the vast majority of his life, Stromness.

Brown's upbringing was relatively secure though not without its challenges. With some exceptions, Brown felt ambivalent at best towards school. He spent much of his time in Stromness Academy bored and felt that elements of schooling set about quashing the imagination rather than letting it run free. Worried by the pressures of making the rent and providing for his family, an air of melancholy often surrounded Brown's father and the anxieties of the household sometimes extended to his young son. Despite this, Brown enjoyed a stable childhood – he had many friends, enjoyed playing football and what his family may have sometimes lacked in a material sense, they more than made up for with love.

The innocence, stability and safety that marked Brown's early childhood was stripped away in his teenage years. When he was 15, Brown was struck down by measles, which left both physical and mental scars; bouts of depression would intermittently haunt him for the rest of his life. Moreover, the outbreak of the Second World War and the stationing of the British Navy Home Fleet at Scapa Flow brought people and activity to Orkney on a scale perhaps never seen before. One of the men involved in the Herculean war effort on Orkney's shores was Brown's father, who worked as a lookout. In the summer of 1940, John suffered a heart attack and died. That same summer, Brown left school and took a job in a Royal Mail sorting office. Perhaps Brown's most pertinent challenge of all, however, arrived in 1941 when, aged 19, he was diagnosed with tuberculosis, at that time both incurable and the leading cause of death amongst young Scots. It was, quite literally, a death sentence.

Following the first of many spells in Eastbank Hospital, a sanitorium in Kirkwall, Brown was discharged yet not cured. The illness which had sought to further isolate him from society meant that doctors confidently predicted that Brown would never be physically able to lead whatever would be conventionally deemed to be a 'normal' life. In a sense, they were right.

Whilst his illness prevented Brown from doing many things, it enabled vicarious reading. He spent much of the next few years in bed – he was, in his own words 'unemployed and unemployable' – and being looked after by his doting mother. In a great twist of fortune for Brown, the poet and academic Frances Scarfe was billeted with the Brown household while stationed as a soldier on Orkney. Scarfe widened Brown's cultural horizons, nurturing an interest in writers including T S Eliot and T E Lawrence. Moreover, Scarfe critiqued the poetry that Brown had started to produce in a serious manner. During this period, Brown engaged with texts and writers that stayed with him for the rest of his life: *The Orkneyinga Saga* ignited a spark of interest in mythic Orkney that never extinguished; Edwin Muir showed him that there was room for Orkney-inspired poetry in contemporary literature; and Graham Greene facilitated a growing interest in Catholicism.

In 1944, Brown found employment at *The Orkney Herald*. Working as Stromness correspondent presented Brown with a number of opportunities: he engaged with local politics and was introduced to the broader Orkney readership for the first time (Margaret Tait, fellow Orcadian and filmmaker, would recall reading these articles 'with pleasure, so glad to see evidence of a writer in our midst'). Whilst some may have been tempted to tiptoe around local issues and local readers in a small community, some of Brown's writings for *The Orkney Herald* at this time zing with firmly held and fiercely expressed opinions, with the Conservative Party and those he identified as the land-owning merchant classes being regular recipients of his ire.

Although Brown had managed to make a name for himself within Orkney through his local journalism, his literary ambitions could never be satisfied by non-fiction. Throughout the 1940s, Brown developed his poetic voice and was published several times in *The New Shetlander*, a literary magazine, towards the end of the decade. Reading some of these poems now, they are demonstrative of what Brown was at the time –

an inexperienced poet and a fairly naïve young man. Still, there are flashes of the style that would become typical of his work and he was beginning to interrogate some of the themes – community, nature, religion – that marked his work throughout his career. Encouraged, too, by fellow Orkney writers such as Ernest Marwick and Robert Rendall, Brown began to find his voice as a poet.

In 1951, Brown was accepted to study at Newbattle Abbey, an adult education college near Edinburgh, where Edwin Muir had recently accepted a position as Warden. Brown's time there, amongst like-minded students and expert tuition, further facilitated his literary development. Although Brown's study was interrupted by bouts of ill-health, its impact on him both as a writer and as a person was significant: in his own words, Newbattle gave Brown 'a sense of purpose and direction'. Buoyed by his time away from Orkney, Brown published his debut poetry collection, *The Storm*, to local acclaim in 1954. The 300 copies printed quickly sold out.

Brown soon returned south, this time to study English Literature at Edinburgh University. Here, he developed relationships with those at the heart of the Edinburgh literary scene, a group perhaps more commonly known as 'the Rose Street poets'. Although trepidatious by nature, Brown was soon assimilated into a social set that was powered by discussion and drinking – his enthusiasm for the latter facilitated the former. Brown revelled in the company and quickly made friends: Sydney Goodsir Smith was a 'kind, gentle man', Hugh MacDiarmid 'showed nothing but encouragement and goodwill' and Norman MacCaig was a 'generous host' of regular house parties. Though Brown developed a number of friends who moved in literary circles throughout his life, he never fully belonged to a particular literary group in either a personal or professional capacity. Arguably, his positioning outwith such circles has helped, rather than hindered, his reputation.

Without doubt, though, the most important relationship that Brown formed in Edinburgh was with Stella Cartwright. Sixteen years Brown's junior, Cartwright – beautiful, intelligent and cultured – infatuated Brown; according to Brown, she awakened in him 'a delight I had not known before'. From the outset, Brown and Cartwright may have made an unlikely pair: Cartwright, a privately-educated, extroverted city woman; Brown, shy, sickly and Orkney to the soles of his feet. However, both were marked by differing forms of innocence, sensitivity and vulnerability. They supported one another in mutual affection, becoming engaged for a very brief spell in 1960. When the relationship broke down, Brown was distraught. The pair kept in touch until Cartwright's untimely death in 1985.

Brown's second collection of poetry, *Loaves and Fishes*, was published in 1959. Following health challenges and a doomed attempt at teacher training, Brown re-enrolled at Edinburgh University, this time to undertake postgraduate research on Gerard Manley Hopkins.

Brown was received into the Catholic Church in 1961. This was the natural result of a long-held interest in Catholicism, with Brown having practised as a Catholic since the fifties. Religious themes had been present throughout Brown's literary career – his opening poem, 'For the Islands I Sing', in his debut collection refers to Scotland as a 'Knox-ruined nation that poet and Saint must rebuild with their passion'. As Brown honed his literary voice, his faith became increasingly central to his work.

His conversion to Catholicism has been behind both biographical (Ron Ferguson, *The Wound and the Gift*, 2011) and scholarly (Linden Bicket, *George Mackay Brown and the Scottish Catholic Imagination*, 2017) publications. In the latter, the author suggests that, such is the centrality of Brown's faith to his writing, his 'work can be read as an excellent case study of the neglected Catholic writer'.[1]

Having graduated from University, Brown returned to Orkney – this time permanently – in 1964. His third collection, *The Year of the Whale*, was published in 1965, elevating his literary reputation to levels hitherto unreached. Warm reviews were followed by several commissions, this time by national publications.

The success of *The Year of the Whale* brought Brown both economic stability and creative freedom. His first short story collection, *A Calendar of Love*, arrived in 1967, quickly followed by *A Time to Keep* in 1969, the year in which a collection of essays, *An Orkney Tapestry*, was also published. Brown's first drama, *A Spell for Green Corn*, was published in 1970 and his first novel, *Greenvoe*, in 1972.

Brown spent his remaining years in Stromness, where a strict writing routine helped to power his prolific literary output. Over these decades, literary awards and recognition were never in short supply: honorary degrees from both Glasgow and Dundee Universities, the Katherine Mansfield Short Story

---

1 Linden Bicket, *George Mackay Brown and the Scottish Catholic Imagination* (2017), p.178.

Prize and an OBE (1974), to name a few. Although physical and mental health challenges lingered, Brown lived his remaining years in comfort in Stromness, his local, national and international reputation further cemented with each passing publication.

Brown published, compilations excepted, 13 poetry collections, nine short story collections, two plays and six novels, the final of which, *Beside the Ocean of Time*, was shortlisted for the 1994 Booker Prize and judged Scottish Book of the Year by the Saltire Society. In addition, Brown penned eight essay collections, a posthumously published autobiography and three collections of children's stories. He wrote a weekly column in The Orcadian right up until his death.

The impact of this body of work still reverberates today. Major scholarly and biographical studies have added to our understanding of Brown in recent decades, Polygon published new editions of several of his works in 2019 and his short stories are included in the Higher English syllabus in Scottish schools. In the first major appraisal of Brown's work, published in 1978, Alan Bold argues that Brown's 'work is beautifully shaped for survival'. Time would appear to be proving him right, arguably propelled by the refusal of Brown's work to be pigeon-holed. In *The History of Orkney Literature* (2010), Simon Hall proposes that 'Brown occupies a progressive position in the literature of his own islands, while at the same time establishing a relevant place for himself within Scottish and international fiction and poetry which advances significantly from the ideals of the writers of the Scottish Renaissance'. In order to achieve this, it could be argued that Brown had to, as Brian Murray suggests in *Interrogation of Silence: The Writings of George Mackay Brown* (2004),'stand outside his own community, by his vision, his illness and his religion'. In this sense, Brown's relative isolation from any literary tribe or trend facilitated the true independence of his imagination and, consequently, the independence of his writing.

At the end of his autobiography, Brown mused on some of his great themes – renewal and the passing of time – whilst implicitly considering his place within Orkney's history:

> there are mysterious marks on the stone circle of Brodgar in Orkney, and on the stones of Skarabrae village, from 5,000 years ago. We will never know what they mean. I am making marks with a pen on a paper, that will have no meaning 5,000 years from now. A mystery abides. We move from silence into silence, and there is a brief stir inbetween, every person's attempt to make a meaning of life and time.

In years to come, Brown's work will continue to have meaning. What that meaning is and who it means something to is, of course, forever unknown. One day, his works may stand, like the stones which proudly populate Orkney's landscape, as monuments to an Orkney and a people that once existed, his work, and his words, like the final utterance to nurses on his deathbed, translating into myth.

An Orkney Worlding: George Mackay Brown's Poetics as Waymarkers for Navigating the Anthropocene

Cáit O'Neill McCullagh

> *I have tried to make a kind of profile of Orkney, which*
> *is not a likeness of today only; it has been worked on*
> *for many centuries.*[1]

This chapter is an invitation to consider the continuing significance of aspects of George Mackay Brown's writing as resources for contemporary readers facing the challenges of this Anthropocene age.[2] Here, the proposal is that Brown's literary voice resonates with the concerns of present-day commentators, activists and scholars who argue that our own juncture in deep time is characterised by the inextricable entanglement of climate crisis with the persistent paradigm of growth-based progress. It is an opportunity to review the present-day significance of a writer who composed poetic connection between a ninth century 'tribe of fisher[s]...in flight from starvation, pestilence, turbulent neighbours' and a mythic dragon; incarnate as a 'black pentecostal' [sic] fire, the outcome and downfall of modernity.[3] Brown's integrative

---

1 George Mackay Brown and Sylvia Wishart, *An Orkney Tapestry* (1969), p.11.

2 During the approximately 11,000 years referred to by scholars as the Holocene period, human ways of living have generated changes across landscapes, lifeways and expressions of languages-in-culture. For millennia, changes occurred at relatively slow rates allowing for periods of stability. Since the eighteenth century, the Anthropocene has been characterised by accelerated, unidirectional anthropogenic progress.

3 George Mackay Brown, *Fishermen With Ploughs* (1971), n.p.

imaginaries are augurs for our era of 'omnicide'[4] threatened through myriad means including global conflict; food insecurity, and forced migrations. True, Brown's largely Orkney-centred works, if read from more metropolitan worldviews, may appear to have little, if any, bearing on these globalised cataclysms. Indeed, his work epitomises the distillation of a specific education in attention to his 'Own': Orkney's 'rhythms of land and sea'; its farmers and fishers, and 'the early epics and ballads' of his mother's Gaelic-speaking ancestors; emanations that he drew upon as if from 'the pure strong rock of [a] spring'.[5] Such radical localism and his focus on the cyclical rhythms of tradition has attracted criticism characterising his repertoire as somewhat static.[6] For some, Brown is too easily positioned as a writer who lived almost his entire life in his island birthplace – within metres from the first house he could remember, 'in a sea-close' between the North Atlantic and the North Sea.[7] How could such a person participate in making the world's history, including its futures? Might someone who died a quarter of a century past – who told readers that his work had been to rescue the 'treasure'[8] of the centuries preceding his birth – speak into our increasingly rapid compression of the dimensions of space and time?[9] Could a writer whose historic 'poetic and ethical mission'

---

4 Levene and Conversi define 'omnicide' as a response to the scientific assessment that the '"developed" world's … economics, technologies, socio-cultural behaviour [and] fundamental value systems, can no longer be sustained as viable or beneficial' for any form of life on the planet. Mark Levene and Daniele Conversi, 'Subsistence societies, globalisation climate change and genocide: discourses of vulnerability and resilience', *The International Journal of Human Rights*, 13, 8 (2014), p.282.

5 George Mackay Brown, *For the Islands I Sing* ([1997] 2008), pp.6, 30.

6 Roderick Watson, *The Literature of Scotland* (2007), pp.14, 132.

7 Brown, *For the Islands*, p.20.

8 George MacKay *Brown Northern Lights* (2013), p.4.

9 See David Harvey, *The Condition of Postmodernity* (1989), pp.260ff, for an explanation >>

was to work 'for the benefit of his archipelagic homeland, for Scotland, and for humanity in general',[10] still have meaning in an era when billionaires plan for the human abandonment of all our earth homes?[11] The following pages open a portal for us to look again at his intentions.

Brown saw himself both as an 'archivist' of the 'rich squandered cargo' of pasts,[12] and as a future-facing voice; viz his address 'To a Hamnavoe Poet of 2093'. It is this expansive and democratic archiving of pasts, and futures, set adrift through writing, that is available for us now; a commons, resources for imagining the world, both as it was and can be:

> ...a few marks
> From an ancient forgotten time
> A child may read
>
> That not far from the stone
> A well
> Might open for wayfarers[13]

Understanding Brown's works in this way, as intentional, social actions that continue to have meaningful life through

---

>> of the geographer's concept of the truncation of space through globalised rapid communication systems, shrinking our experience of time to an all-pervasive present. For Harvey, this leaves humanity in the situation of having 'to learn to cope with an overwhelming sense of compression of our spatial and temporal worlds' (p.240). Doreen Massey, *A Global Sense of Place* (1991), p.24, refers back to the origin of this concept in Marx's writing about the annihilation of distance through the modern ordering of time.

10 Halszka Leleń, 'Experimenting with Historiographic Narrative and Guidebook Style' in *An Orkney Tapestry* by George Mackay Brown', *Roczniki Humanistyczne*, 67, 11 (2019), p.157.

11 Luke Devlin, Mairi McFadyen, Mike Small *et al.* 'Going to the Moon', *Less:* 1 (1) (2020), p.2.

12 George Mackay Brown, *Northern Lights: A Poet's Sources* (2013), p.4.

13 George Mackay Brown, 'A Work for Poets' in Archie Bevan and Brian Murray (eds), *The Collected Poems of George Mackay Brown* ([1996] 2005).

the connections they inspire, contemporary readers can become allies in his process, putting people in place within the ongoing archive of story, valuing and sharing lived experiences. This is 'worlding'. It is what Brown's fellow archipelago dweller, and thinker, Martinique-born poet/philosopher Édouard Glissant suggests should be a poet's primary work: creating complex and ongoing 'connections between [our] place and the whole, and [diffusing] the whole throughout [our] place'.[14] It is a way of seeing that Brown's friend and brother skald/bard Seamus Heaney understood, recognising it in Brown's ability to communicate 'everything' by passing it through the transformative 'eye of the needle of Orkney'.[15] This making of a world through words: in the activities of writing; reading, and the inspirations that this relationship between writers and their readers kindles, is akin to philosopher Hannah Arendt's description of the ancient concept of poetics, both composed of *poiesis* (fabrication, craft-skill) and *praxis* (thought and speech into critical action).[16] Arendt's view was that poetics, like all actions, are made in relation to other beings. This relationality makes poetic activities boundless; working in continuum, stimulating effects through people, all life, across spaces, and through times.[17] Brown's many modalities of writing are radiant with this way of worlding – forming; being made by, and making connections:

14 Édouard Glissant, 'From the whole-world treatise', *Review: Literature and Arts of the Americas*, 32, 58 (1999), p.32.

15 Seamus Heaney cited in Stromness Library Blogspot 'Seamus Heaney (1939-2013) – Saturday 31 August 2013'.

16 See Maurizio d'Entreves, 'Hannah Arendt', *The Stanford Encyclopedia of Philosophy* (Fall 2019).

17 Hannah Arendt, *The Human Condition* ([1958] 1998), p.189.

Everything we do sets the whole web of
creation trembling, with light or with
darkness…a good word spoken might help
a beggar in Calcutta or a burning child in
Burundi; or conversely. [18]

The remainder of this essay introduces aspects of Brown's
Orkney worlding: expressions of dwelling; empathy; 'co-
becoming', and repair.[19] They are highlighted as waymarkers,
runes 'carved' for us, for our own way of perceiving and
shaping the world through poetics, becoming as poets ourselves in our imagining and assembling of possible futures: [20]

Language unstable as sand, but poets
Strike on hard rock, carving
Rune and hieroglyph…
Keep vigil. The tongues flow yet… [21]

Worlding as Dwelling in 'the intimacies of the home patch'[22]

A *makar* of world imaginaries, Brown certainly appears to have
imbibed the principles of one of his own literary heroes Bertolt
Brecht,[23] whose own manifesto was that writing is, indeed, a

18 Brown, *For the Islands*, p.174.

19 See Bawaka Country et al, 'Goŋ Gurtha: Enacting response-abilities as situated
co-becoming', *Environment and Planning D: Society and Space*, 37, 4 (2019),
pp.682-702.

20 Brown uses this trope in several works to connote the role of the poet. It is an
allusion to a 'skaldic' lineage of skill in knowing and carving/composing with
the runes – the *poiesis* that accompanies the praxis/social actions and elicitive
learning possible in poetry as a dialogue with readers (see Brown, *For the Islands*,
pp.30-1, 139-40).

21 George Mackay Brown, 'To a Hamnavoe Poet of 2093' in Linda Andersson
Burnett (ed), *Archipelagos: Poems from Writing the North* (2014).

22 McCullagh cited in Raghnaid Sandilands, 'Tobar an Dualchais: In praise of B-road
studies', *West Highland Free Press*, 9 May 2020.

23 Brown, *For the Islands*, p.139.

'social action'; 'holding a mirror up' to society to promote critical thinking.[24] In his 'singing'[25] of the everyday of his community and environment, Brown offers situated vignettes viewed through microcosmic lenses,[26] enabling his readers to witness, with him, people negotiating particular responses to the complexities of modernity. Skilfully adopting the vagueness of symbolism,[27] Brown renovates the specific language of Orkney – people and place – into an idiom of universal relation[28]; a translation of the specific through the fundamental cycles of human life.[29] For example, in *Greenvoe*, when Ivan Westray – at one end of, for him, an otherwise familiar journey – looks out into dense sea-fog and proclaims that he is lost, a whole generation is connoted.[30] Brown leads readers from this moment into a redding-up of the skipper's mythic genealogy, offering us the experience of the loss of a story of a people, and their environment, with and through Ivan. Brown's epic poem cycle *Fishermen with Ploughs* is also redolent with this theme, urgent with the significance for people and places of the loss of historicity and environmental integrity.[31]

---

24 John Willet and Ralph Manheim (eds), *Bertolt Brecht: Poems 1913-1956* ([1940] 1979) p.483.

25 After GMB 'Prologue' in George Mackay Brown, *The Storm and Other Poems* (1954), p.9.

26 In his autobiography, Brown discusses the importance of both realism and imagination in the writer's work and communicates his own understanding that his portrayals of Orkney – people and place – afford a microcosm through which both he and his readers can apprehend more global themes and concerns. Brown, *For the Islands*, p.168.

27 See Anthony P Cohen, 'Segmentary knowledge: a Whalsay sketch', in Mark Hobart (ed), *An anthropological critique of development: The growth of ignorance* (1993), p.21.

28 Glissant, 'From the whole-world treatise', pp.33-4.

29 Leleń, 'Experimenting with Historiographic Narrative and Guidebook Style', p.157.

30 George Mackay Brown, *Greenvoe* (1972), p.20.

31 'After Ullrich Kockel, "Reflexive traditions and heritage production"' in Ullrich Kockel and Máiréad Nic Criath (eds), *Cultural Heritages as Reflexive Traditions* (2007), p.39.

In these works, Brown's thesis comes close to what ethnologist Ullrich Kockel has characterised as 'the eviction of the folk from their rightful place in history... by the hegemony' through the non-democratic pursuit of top-down progress.[32] For the folk of Brown's fictive Rackwick and imagined Greenvoe such progress makes them strangers in their own places. We see this theme nuanced in the poem 'The Drowning Brothers'.[33] Here, Brown uses the 'silver tongue' of the burn, as a metaphor for the constancy and dynamism of community and environment in synergy (a common motif in Brown's writing),[34] to signify sharp contrast with the distant, disengaged throb of a tractor.[35] It is the mechanics of disengagement that Brown decries; forms of progress that privilege dominant rather than connective relations between people, and between people and places. It is a tendency towards instrumentalism that he traces back even to Rackwick's earliest settlers instrumental deployment of 'oxen and millstones and bronze throats of agriculture'.[36] As readers, we feel the wrench as people's culture becomes estranged from their co-natural relations with the earth.

To effect this disruption, often Brown brings readers to meet his characters first amid the continuum of their everyday lives and relations:

> Small gestures...
> he would go to the crags
> Each morning...

---

32 Ullrich Kockel, 'Putting the Folk in Their Place: Tradition, Ecology and the Public Role of Ethnology', *Anthropological Journal of European Cultures* 17, 1 (2008), p.8.

33 Brown, *Fishermen With Ploughs*, pp.73-4.

34 Brown, *For the Islands*, p.140.

35 Brown, *Fishermen With Ploughs*, p.73-4.

36 Brown, *Fishermen With Ploughs*, n.p.

For a clutch of eggs...

And she to the burn with her pail...

- On such a tranquil wheel their time

was spun...[37]

In this way, he evokes the reflexive interplay of environments and people, co-forming each other, interweaving the imagery of traditions of what had been, while also intimating the traditions of 'what can be' through people's affective being:[38]

No man is an island, and all that we ever say or

think or do – however seemingly unremarkable

– may set the whole web of existence trembling

and affect the living and the dead and the unborn.[39]

Brown understands the both/and of community (relational, collaborative dwelling), and the significance of the individual; the way that each person 'may be touched...with the music of the spheres':[40]

[T]he life of everyone is unique and

mysterious. Under all the

accumulation of custom, boredom

and drift lies somewhere the

'immortal diamond' [41]

---

37 Brown, 'Twins' (1971), p.44.

38 After Ariella Azoulay, *Potential History* (2019). Azoulay argues that rejection of learning via the transmission of traditional knowledges and wisdom was 'made into an ideal of freedom' in 'the Imperial condition' of modernity (p.320). In this way tradition has been peripheralised and consigned to a finite past.

39 George Mackay Brown, 'No man is an Island', *Weekend Scotsman*, 30 August (1986).

40 Brown, *For the Islands I Sing*, p.168.

41 Brown, *For the Islands*, p.19.

In his autobiography, Brown returns often to distilling and articulating the intention of his work. He clarifies that he believes it is to reveal what is under the 'mask' of history; to speak of a world in which 'the true face dreams on [as] The Fable [sic] is repeated over'.[42] In this, his activity of worlding, Brown's uses of traditional symbolic tropes and themes are not simply unconscious regressions into romanticism. They are repudiations of the directional thrust of certain forms of history; of the reification both events that took place, and also *took place* from people. Contemporary readers might connect this aspect of his poetic praxis with current discourse that promotes ideas of assembling more sustainable and socially just futures through similarly refuting the imperial construction of directional time,[43] the idea that time's arrow flies only forwards.

Professor of culture and creative practitioner, Ariella Azoulay, characterises a more flexible approach to time (like Brown) seeing it as an opening towards 'potential history': 'a form of being with others, both living and dead, across time, against the separation of the past from the present'.[44] For Azoulay, potential history work supports global repair,[45] recovering actions and knowledges consigned to an historical past so that their wisdom remains available; a commons of plural ways of knowing how to dwell in the world.[46] Brown's writing denotes such 'dwelling', expressing cycles of tradition as participations in 'mystery [abiding] from silence into silence', and renewals

42 Brown, *An Orkney Tapestry*, p.11.

43 See Priya Satia, *Time's Monster: How History Makes History* (2020), p.3, on the unintended consequences of modernity's project of progress 'the detritus of empire in the form of climate crisis, global inequalities... [of] modern imperialism... grounded in a vision of history understood as necessarily progress oriented'.

44 Azoulay, *Potential History*, p.43.

45 Azoulay, *Potential History*, pp.530ff.

46 Azoulay, *Potential History*, p.320.

of these as stirrings in that silence: 'every person's attempt to make a meaning of life and time'.[47] These worlding poetics also sit well alongside anthropologist David Graeber's thesis that 'the ultimate, hidden truth of the world is that it is something that we make, and could just as easily make differently'.[48]

To invite readers into the 'richness and uniqueness'[49] of his distinct portraits of people-places through times; the universally 'immortal diamond'.[50] Brown cultivated his writing as a dialogue both with community and environment.[51] For him, writing was no insular act.[52] Rather, in cherishing the intimacies of his home patch, tilling that miniscule portion of land,[53] he drew on a treasury of familiar, indeed *familial*, sources (Norse mythology, Gaelic traditions and biblical texts) to elicit themes that he himself owned were rarely new.[54] In attending to county and parochial concerns, Brown's writing resembles that of his near contemporary, Irish author Patrick Kavanagh. Each, writing individually, established their works as praxes of sowing and nurturing the ground of *commonplace* being as the

47 Brown, *For the Islands*, p.168.

48 David Graeber, *The Utopia of Rules: On Technology, Stupidity, and the Secret Joys of Bureaucracy* (2015), p.39.

49 Brown, *For the Islands*, p.140.

50 Brown borrows this phrase from Gerard Manley Hopkins, whose poetry he admired.

51 I am grateful to Stromnessian academic Rebecca Ford for sharing her thoughts on Brown's writing as an exemplum of Mikhail Bakhtin's dialogism in which 'the word' given 'in language is half someone else's'. *Mikhail Bakhtin, The Dialogic Imagination: Four Essays* (1981), p.293 cited in Rebecca Ford, 'Weaving Words: a dialogical approach to creativity and community discourse in Orkney', unpublished presentation (2016).

52 Brown, *For the Islands*, pp.26-7, 166, including the writer's conviction that his story of Magnus, twelfth century earl and saint, must have resonance in the twentieth century. He likens Magnus to theologian Dietrich Bonhoeffer, executed for his opposition to Adolf Hitler.

53 See Watson *The Literature of Scotland* (2007), p.132.

54 Brown, *For the Islands*, p.168.

place in which the universal may also thrive. Each expressed their local ecologies as vital for the radiance of the greater cosmology. We hear this in Kavanagh's announcement with 'bravado [of] the notion that the potato-patch is the ultimate':[55]

> To know fully even one field or one land is a lifetime's experience. In the world of poetic experience, it is depth that counts, not width.[56]

Brown's own cultivation within and for a people and place often characterised as being peripheral; at the 'utmost corners of the warld',[57] shows equal, if more quietly radical, boldness. He persisted in working the ground of each page towards forming narrative and poetic planes where 'famers and fishing-folk, and their work',[58] shared significance with monarchs and mythic heroes. His was an aesthetic and ethics founded in those principles that Kavanagh recognised as the 'right kind of sensitive courage and...sensitive humility' needed to see the universal in the particular, including in the fundamentals of the parish:[59]

> [A]ny small community is a microcosm. It is not necessary to stray very far from your back yard. The whole world gathers about the parish pump.[60]

---

55 Patrick Kavanagh, '"The Parish and the Universe" in Collected Pruse (1967) – extract' in Mark Storey (ed), *Poetry and Ireland since 1800: A Source Book* ([1967], 1988), p.205.

56 Patrick Kavanagh, 'The Parish and the Universe' cited in Robert Macfarlane, '"My Eyes are In My Feet": Introduction' in Nan Shepherd, *The Living Mountain* ([1977] 2011), p.9.

57 From William Fowler's (1560-1612) 'Sonet. In Orknay' in John MacQueen and Tom Scott (eds), *The Oxford Book of Scottish Verse* ([1966] 1989), p.260, l.1.

58 Brown, *For the Islands*, p.26.

59 Kavanagh, 'The Parish and the Universe', p.205.

60 Brown, *For the Islands*, p.168.

Brown's ability both to be in the particular and be worldly is evident in his dexterity with, as Seamus Heaney put it, widening 'the cosmological lens', bringing readers 'beyond the usual' *and* assuring them 'that the terra [is] still firma'.[61] George Mackay Brown found and wove the cosmic mystery of a 'thread too bright for the eye' in the everyday yarns of 'green corn', 'blue fish', and the red of 'rut and rieving and wrath'.[62]

Empathy and *ecocritical* awareness

Such ability in strengthening and expanding the connective tissue between people and places, bound through times in patterns that extend across space – viz *Time in a Red Coat* – is exemplified in what Édouard Glissant conceptualised as the 'poetics of relation'.[63] For Glissant, writing constituted the social action of 'speak[ing]: the world'.[64] Just as Arendt had linked speech to action through their being mutually realised in 'spaces of appearance'- where people disclose their identities in 'reciprocity and solidarity'.[65] Glissant knew that writing a world from one's own ground could also ground one in worldly relations:

> We discover that the place where we live, from which we speak, can no longer be abstracted by us from that mass of energy that hails us from afar. We can no longer grasp...its infinite... sufferings, and pleasures, unless we lash it to... the world's totality.[66]

---

61 Seamus Heaney speaking in 2004, cited in Maggie Fergusson, *George Mackay Brown: The Life* (2006), p.x.

62 Brown, *Fishermen with Ploughs*, p.29 .

63 Édouard Glissant, *Poetics of Relation* (1997).

64 Glissant, *The Treatise of the Whole World*, p.32.

65 d'Entreves, "Hannah Arendt"; see also Arendt *The Human Condition*, pp.199ff.

66 Glissant, *The Treatise of the Whole World*, p.32.

As already intimated, Brown's aesthetic was itself a conscious turning to such otherwise looking. As with Glissant's work, including his evocations of 'archipelago thinking'[67], Brown's writing also expresses an integrative and empathetic world-view, embracing the paradox of insularity amid multiple archipelagic connections. In Brown's islands, edges both are defined and infinitely open; mirrored materially and poetically in the opposite rhythms of land and sea, which for Brown were a continuous meeting of diverse forms in patterned 'harmony'.[68] George Mackay Brown's was a vision of being emplaced in the world whilst also refuting the idea of exceptionalism; both able to:

> ...rent and till a narrow patch
> Not much bigger than my coat[69]

and to mobilise the connectivity of land and ocean

> From the black furrow, a fecund
> Whisper of dust,
> From the gray furrow, a sudden
> Gleam and thrust,
> Crossings of net and ploughshare,
> Fishbone and crust.[70]

This is the view of the 'Beachcomber', who, in Brown's eponymous poem, encounters the multiplicity of the world's materials brought to his shore.[71] In this poem, as in his life,

---

67 Michael Wiedorn *Think Like an Archipelago: Paradox in the Work of Edouard Glissant* (2017).

68 Brown, *Fishermen with Ploughs*, p.38.

69 George Mackay Brown, 'Eynhallow: Crofter and Monastery' (2005), p.171.

70 Brown 'Black Furrow, Gray Furrow' (1971), p.38.

71 Brown, *Fishermen with Ploughs*, p.63.

Brown situates himself at the ebb, ready to welcome stories from 'under the horizon'.[72] Just as the beachcomber's mirror poet, Derek Walcott – a St Lucia-born, and archipelago dwelling descendent of Empire-entangled forebears – wrote it. Brown knew 'that the sea is history'.[73] This connective perspective is key for contemporary living. We are still navigating the legacies of that globalisation, which was announced for Brown's 'Beachcomber' with the arrival of 'barrel[s] of sodden oranges' from Spanish shipwrecks by The Kame.[74] For contemporary shore watchers the metaphor and the experience extends to the plastics made in China that spill onto the beach at Eathie. Brown's exemplification of the connective *and* connecting perspective of beachcombing, at a sifting rather than impenetrable edge, continues to waymark a condition of worldly empathy. Like Walcott, Brown was also a child of the Empire,[75] imbided with an early learning of how the sea embodies relational potential; its dissolution of edges remained with him as a geo-poetical metaphor for his own and other's complex identities, including hybridity.

In his archipelago, and in the world, Brown owned this plurality. He experienced it in the ancestral flows of Lowland Scots' and Highland Gaels' legacies of economics and migrations that were united in his parents.[76] It is this perspective that gave criticality to his reading of those authorised, epic versions of history; promotions of forms of progress that would induce 'states of most depressing quiescence' in their

---

72 Brown, *For the Islands*, p.168.

73 Derek Walcott, *Collected Poems: 1948-1984x*, (1986), p.364.

74 Brown, *Fishermen with Ploughs*, p.63.

75 Brown, *For the Islands*, p.23.

76 Brown, *For the Islands*, p.9ff.

effects.[77] Reaching through times and across spaces, he forged creative and intellectual links based on the constant centrality of lived experiences. He proposed an imagined resonance in the work of being and making a world between the oral tradition bearers who stored and shared the Border ballads and Nobel Laureate Thomas Mann; between poets and plumbers.[78] Interrupting and connecting, Brown's poetic inclination to synergy between particulars, evident in the many threads elucidated in his poem 'Shroud'[79] or the adaptive, anticipatory, collective weaving of the settling community in 'The Net',[80] connotes the necessary multiplicity of skills, experiences, and identities that compose the 'orchestra' of community.[81]

Engaging with Brown's representations of populated environments offers contemporary readers an opportunity to experience his poetics as ecocritical engagements.[82] Following Brown's model of observing and interpreting people's interactions and perceptions in context – both with and in their environments and cultures – readers may be inspired not only to recognise, but also reflect and interact critically and creatively with their own anticipations and responses to our present-day ecological crises. 'This lively possibility is afforded because Brown's ecological engagement is holistic. His writing mobilises people's historicities along with their

---

77 Brown, 'In Days to Come', 'Island Diary', *Orkney Herald*, 9 September 1952.

78 Brown, *For the Islands*, p.31.

79 Brown, *Fishermen with Ploughs*, p.29.

80 Brown, *Fishermen with Ploughs*, p.9.

81 Brown, *For the Islands*, p.11.

82 See Marjan Shokouhi, 'Towards a poetics of dwelling: Patrick Kavanagh's countryside', *Estudios Irlandeses*, 14(1 (2020) , p.14, for a detailed discussion on ecocriticism in literary theory.

everyday culture as lenses for viewing the impact of imposed progress on their ways of being in the world. He evokes his own empathy and invokes ours:

> I'm so desperately involved with all the weak things, lonely things, suffering things I see about me. I can't bear the pity I feel for them... The world's a torture chamber... It seems most folk can live with that kind of thing. Not me – I get all caught up in it.[83]

In 'Celia', one of the stories assembled in *A Time to Keep*, Brown, the very writer who composed the exquisite, romantic poesy of 'the buttered bannock of the moon',[84] a flame in that 'fire of images'[85] recited, since, by at least two generations of Orcadian's 'singing' their islands in his words,[86] lays open a harrowing seam of pain. The 'blood everywhere' that Celia decries in the suffering things around her is a notable flow throughout Brown's oeuvre. Just as he galvanises the lyricality of the intertwining 'deep marvellous rhythms of sea and land, darkness and light',[87] Brown's metaphysical representations of nature's possibility, rendered in motifs such as the ever changing music of a Highland burn,[88] are also interleaved with

---

83 George Mackay Brown, *A Time to Keep and Other Stories*, (1969), p.15-16.

84 George Mackay Brown, 'Hamnavoe' in Archie Bevan and Brian Murray (eds), *The Collected Poems of George Mackay Brown* ([1996] 2005), p.25.

85 Brown, 'Hamnavoe'.

86 See Brown, *For the Islands*, p.17, where he alludes to the intimacy between song and poetry, which he believed he had imbibed through the relict legacy of his mother's ancestors: an antiquity of the Gaelic oral tradition and its 'legends and songs as old as Homer perhaps' (p.15). Brown extends this appreciation of musicality and language in tradition to his reading of the complexities of being in a community, comparing it to playing in an orchestra (p.11).

87 George Mackay Brown, *Letters from Hamnavoe*, (1975), p.67.

88 See Brown, *For the Islands*, p.140, for the poet's description of the Highland Burn as a metaphor for culture in flow, outwith perimeters of time or space.

his acknowledgement of the 'common soiling of the world', its 'sewer of pain'.[89] His own cultural hybridity may have increased his sensitivity to such apparent paradoxes. It is, of course, also an intimation of his closeness to the fundamentals of being;[90] ultimately, the generative source for his plaintive mediations of environmental pain.

Scholar of sustainability studies, Glenn Albrecht, has recently refined his own theoretical concept for explaining why it is that he thinks people, like Brown, express such environmental, and cultural sensitivity, even to the point of embodying the pain they perceive. To help describe the phenomenon he has identified and observed, he has coined the term 'solastalgia'.[91] For Albrecht, solastalgia is composed of 'the distress that is produced by environmental change impacting on people while they are directly connected to their home environment'.[92] It is pain induced through lack of solace. Unlike its close relation, nostalgia, solastalgia is not an experience borne out of separation from home, including the imagination of a better home that is past. It is a 'negative earth emotion' situated in everyday relations in and towards home, while also not feeling at home in the world.[93] For Albrecht, accepting that solastalgia is a legitimate response to the precarity caused by the abrasions of the Anthropocene is key to understanding the 'emotional and cultural dimensions of the human relationship

89 Brown, 'Hamnavoe'.

90 Halszka Leleń, 'Orcadian Poetics of Hope: Lyrical Dimensions and (Ex)tensions of the Topos in the Poetry of George Mackay Brown', *Ethos*, 32(4), (2019), p.157.

91 Glenn Albrecht, 'Negating Solastalgia: An Emotional Revolution from the Anthropocene to the Symbiocene', *American Imago*, 77 (1), (2020), p.9.

92 Albrecht, 'Negating Solastalgia', p.9.

93 Albrecht, 'Negating Solastalgia', p.9.

to land'.[94] It is also a necessary condition for attending to changes and losses in the waymarkers, signs and symbols, for 'a healthy ecosystem and place'.[95] Albrecht praises those writers whom he sees as having expressed early warnings 'about the biophysical and emotional implications' of ecological distress.[96] Making the condition of solastalgia known is an important step towards countering its causes.[97] Through the writings of authors who stay committed to both environment and neighbours, Albrecht suggests, a common emotional and political purpose is inspired. Repair becomes possible through accepting their mirroring of 'the love of the totality of our place relationships, and a willingness to accept the political responsibility for protecting and conserving them at all scales'.[98]

Certainly, contemporary readers of Brown's works will have little difficulty in finding both the symptoms and the creative possibilities of solastalgia in his words. Brown spent a lifetime close to the elements that Orkney's northern climate embraces.[99] He understood the depths of those winters of 'death ... dank and cold' rendered in fellow Orcadian, Robert Rendall's *Renewal*; a sonnet that he claimed was 'one of the most perfect' he knew.[100] He also lived alongside crofters engaged in the challenging yearly cycles of 'burnishing... seed from snow',[101] and fishers who were 'up to the thwart in

---

94 Albrecht, 'Negating Solastalgia', p.13.
95 Albrecht, 'Negating Solastalgia', p.14.
96 Albrecht, 'Negating Solastalgia', p.17.
97 Albrecht, 'Negating Solastalgia', p.20.
98 Albrecht, Negating Solastalgia', p.20
99 For example, see Brown, *Letters from Hamnavoe*, pp.76-7.
100 Brown, *For the Islands*, p.67.
101 Brown, *Letters from Hamnavoe*, p.50.

haddocks';[102] dual roles taken on by individuals active in Orkney's subsistence economies for millennia. It is this belonging both to place and people that imbues Brown's literary exposures of ecological pain with the complex synergies both of cultural and natural stress.[103]

Repair – dwelling in co-becoming

For contemporary commentators, accepting the indivisibility of culture and nature is a necessary critique of the dominant paradigm in which 'scientific' and 'social' wisdom are different; an imposed duality used to construct knowledge systems useful for modernity.[104] Brown's poetics anticipated such a retournement to more holistic ways of knowing, nurtured in our intimate interrelationship with the 'whole web of creation', cognisant that every action sets the web 'trembling'.[105] This 'poetics of hope' a synergy of lyrical juxtapositions and under-statement encouraging readers to seek waymarkers of optimism scattered through his tales of individuals facing adversities.[106] Brown attributed his aesthetic and ethos to his Roman Catholicism.[107] It was also contextualised by his formation in the intermingling genealogies of his Scots-

---

102 Brown, *Letters from Hamnavoe*, p.41.

103 In *Fishermen with Ploughs*, Brown sets forth an imagined millennium of settle-ment, displacement and recursive migration in, from and to Rackwick, in the island of Hoy, an island he visited regularly, and through which he connected to the universality of people-place experiences (see Brown, *For the Islands*, p.73.) Brown filled *Fishermen with Ploughs* with motifs that both connote the adaptiv-ity and the pains undertaken by people experiencing displacement by the 'dead[ening] fires' of an unchecked, processual modernity (see Brown, *For the Islands*, pp.163-4).

104 See Rodney Harrison, 'Beyond "Natural" and "Cultural" Heritage: Toward an Ontological Politics of Heritage in the Age of Anthropocene', *Heritage and Society*, 8 (1), (2015), pp.24–42.

105 Brown, *For the Islands*, p.174.

106 Leleń, 'Orcadian Poetics of Hope', p.157.

107 For example see Brown, *For the Islands*, pp.172-3.

Orcadian and Gael heritages, and attuned through 'the eye of the needle of Orkney'.

This complex ontology – Brown's knowledges for ways of being – composed of spiritual and traditional wisdoms, and Brown's emplaced awareness, resembles articulations of indigenous knowledge systems elsewhere in the world. It is close to the concepts of 'co-becoming', an holistic worldview of the Goŋ Gurtha in the continent named by Europeans as Australia.[108] Goŋ Gurtha, Indigenous people of Yolŋu (Northeast Arnhem Land) describe their worldly co-becoming as a kinship network with all life; 'dwelling' in 'complex and uncertain places. Paying attention and listening to more-than-human worlds' and 're-learning...in relation with others – whose essence – we cannot know'.[109] For Goŋ Gurtha, as it was often for Brown, this way of being is transmitted in music. Brown, brought such musicality into the dialogue of his writing, expressing the 'music of the spheres', 'the Highland burn', and the 'low contented croon' of his maternal home.[110] For Goŋ Gurtha, this dialogue is expressed and experienced through song spirals 'rich and multi-layered articulations, passed down through the generations and sung...to make and remake the lifegiving connections between people and place.[111] In Brown's poem 'Hamnavoe', (both an elegy both for his father and his birthplace home), the fluidity of his facility for singing such music across the indivisibility of nature and culture is subtle and rich:

> The kirk, in a gale of psalms, went heaving through
> A tumult of roofs, freighted for heaven.

108 Bawaka Country *et al*, 'Goŋ Gurtha: Enacting response-abilities'
109 Bawaka Country *et al*, 'Goŋ Gurtha: Enacting response-abilities', p.693.
110 Brown, *For the Islands*, pp.168, 140, 27.
111 Bawaka Country *et al*, 'Goŋ Gurtha: Enacting response-abilities', p.683.

And lovers unblessed by steeples, lay under
The buttered bannock of the moon.[112]

This is indeed writing drawn out of the 'strong rock of the spring...somehow akin to the blood in our veins and to the ebbings and floods of the sea'[113]. Brown's poetics of relational 'co-becoming', set alongside contemporary writing concerning the significance of traditional wisdoms and indigenous worldviews – long occluded by metropolitan and imperialist positioning – offers a new frame through which contemporary readers can view him. Brown's panegyrics to Orkney's 'magic'[114] and his expressions of 'negative earth emotions' – legitimate responses to a complex Anthropocene – attain radical significance as disclosures not only of his identity, but of his intention: poiesis and praxis as waymarkers towards worldly repair and future assembling. Central to his writing is this deep understanding of the constancy of renewal; a far from regressive cycle of renovation both through change and also through sustainment:

The birds return...
The waters rise...
Come, dancer, go
Step by circle
The reel endures.[115]

In reviewing Brown's writing, exploring aspects of his relational empathy for the people-place in the world that he was given to share his 'co-becoming' with, we can begin to

---

112 Brown, 'Hamnavoe', p.171.
113 Brown, *For the Islands*, p.30.
114 George Mackay Brown, *Let's See the Orkney Islands*, (1948), p.47.
115 Brown, 'Old Man' (1971), p.66

appreciate his work as an active ethnology. As a detailed and comparative study of people and culture, Brown's writing denotes both his observation and analysis of the granular and the universally resonant; connective tissue that roots people in expansive relations from their own homes into the world. Interpreting what people around him were doing, in the contexts of their environments and historicities,[116] Brown placed himself both in and apart; the between both of the hybrid and also, according to philosopher Merleau-Ponty, of the 'Own' ethnologist.[117] For Merleau-Ponty, this is the position of someone open to the experience of transforming their thinking:

> We become ethnologists of our own society if we
> distance ourselves from it... [This is] a way of thinking
> that demands that we transform ourselves.[118]

In considering our contemporary reading of Brown, this is an important point. As already intimated in this chapter, far from being narrowly tethered – limited spatially and temporally – George Mackay Brown's 'Orkney worlding' was, and continues to be a social act of proposing ways of living that have been possible and, through our ongoing co-becoming through times, with all being and, across space, of what can be possible; 'birds return', and the 'reel endures'. It is a way of seeing that requires transformation, a stepping aside from one's 'Own' in order to see it closely, and in close relation to the world. For Brown, he chose to exercise this empathetic ethnology

116 After Ullrich Kockel, 'Reflexive Traditions and Heritage Production', in Ullrich Kockel and Mairead Nic Craith (eds) *Cultural Heritages as Reflexive Traditions*. (2007), p.39.

117 Maurice Merleau-Ponty, *Signs* (1964) p.120.

118 Merleau-Ponty, *Signs*, p.120.

creatively, in a poetics of relation: as poet, playwright, journalist, novelist and essayist. Yet, he saw no separation between these activities, his ways of worlding, and those of fishers, farmers, and plumbers.[119] This expansive aspect of his world view, resonates with philosopher Antonio Gramsci's belief that when we think critically we are becoming philosophers, continues in Orkney today.[120] The recent coming together of boat builders, songwriters, farmers, museum curators, artists and others in the practice research-based *New Connections Across the Northern Isles* project is one iteration of this. Joining across their islands to co-curate their maritime cultures in films and new writing, [121] and to reflect together on how to sustain archipelago lives and livings, these 'new connecters' shared their own 'creative ethnologies'[122]; drawing on the resources of their historical cultures and traditions, of land and sea to continue co-becoming towards the traditions of what can be.[123]

While it is not possible to draw a direct line from Brown's works to these expressions of renovation, renewal, and relationality, traces of his poiesis resonate in these new creative ethnologies of people living in Orkney today. Here, for example, are the words of Sarah Jane Gibbon, Orcadian, historian, archaeologist, song collector and composer of her

119 Brown, *For the Islands*, p.31.

120 Quentin Hoare and Geoffrey Nowell Smith (eds), *Antonio Gramsci. Selections from the Prison Notebooks of Antonio Gramsci* (1971), p.330.

121 New Connections 'New Connections Across the Northern Isles' (2019) online: https://irc.hw.ac.uk/new-connections.html

122 For a discussion of the emergent field of 'creative ethnologies', originating in Scotland, see Ullrich Kockel, and Mairi McFadyen, 'On the carrying stream into the European mountain: Roots and routes of creative (Scottish) ethnology', *Anuac*, 8(2) (2019), pp.189-211.

123 See Azoulay, *Potential History*, p.320.

people and place, as shared in one of the *New Connections* project's short films:

> I always store within my head that idea of the footsteps of the folk that have gone before us, and how many different people have walked here and lived here; fished from here, how many other people will have died on this coast…it's much, much more than a single event…we have a Norse farmstead just along the coast. We have a chapel. We have a broch. We have stories of giants. They're all there, just at this piece of coast… we're looking out on that waves and minding that folk mak a living on the sea. They're all using this piece of coast, and they all have different perceptions of it.[124]

Brown understood that in the metaphorical rune-carving of his work he was stepping for some time from silence into the music of the spheres; joining in co-becoming, part of a collaborative orchestra of being, in order to contribute his marks to making the way for all living in the world. Sarah Jane's ebb-rooted and world-facing creative ethnology may well be one of the plurality of emanations transmitted, heard, and reflected upon 'not far from the stone' at which Brown carved his words. She too is a child of Orkney, and in her childhood had access to the 'well' of wisdom and sustainment that Brown kept 'open for wayfarers'.[125] We might imagine them both co-becoming in this particular *and* connected continuum of relations. For all of us stepping into the Highland

124 New Connections (2019) 'Songs of People, Sea and Place' online: https://vimeo.com/showcase/5946154/video/326204661

125 Brown, 'A Work for Poets' (2005), p.378.

burn, reading George Mackay Brown, today, the indices of his waymarking – with and for people, emplaced around this world – can offer a way for our own rooting, cultivating, anticipating, and worlding empathetic futures; the potential histories of what and who we can become together.

Notes of a Failed Nature Writer

Alison Miller

What was I thinking when I came back home to Orkney seven years ago? I'd spent the best part of my adult life and the whole of my professional life in Glasgow. But I'd been trying to get home for years. And when I finally moved into a newly built house looking out on Houton Bay and Scapa Flow, I thought I'd made it.

Made it to the long light nights of summer, the short dark days of winter. Made it to the shifting grey and blue, turquoise and silver of the sea; to the high bright skies and majestic clouds; to the sea cliffs and the waves crashing below; to wild flowers quivering in crevices of rock; to wind so strong it can knock you off your feet; to days so calm the sea is shot silk; to birds reclaiming the Orkney names I knew as a bairn – skeldro, dunter, whaap, teeack, Solan goose, Tammie Norrie, mallimak; to rooms brimming with sea-glitter and Northern light. All the light I needed to find my way. All the light I needed to write by.

What was I thinking?

In all that time I was away, Orkney had pared itself down in my imagination to its elemental bones. I was as bad as any tourist, romanticising island life, idealising it. I'd bought the version repackaged for the jaded metropolitan. Yet, I was born here, grew up here, experienced as much angst and alienation as the next teenager. Couldn't wait to get away. In my long absence, I lost family – a brother, my father, my mother – to death; others to illness and irreconcilable differences. And yet, I couldn't wait to get back.

When I came home, I told myself, I would spend my days roaming the shore, picking up shells, stones, shards of china and glass; going back to my desk at a bright sea-facing window and writing, writing. I didn't consider how much loss there was to face, how much grief. It didn't occur to me that I would feel like an outsider in the community I had landed in, that I would struggle to find my feet.

How to reconcile my love of the sea, the shore, of the fluent lines of the Orkney landscape, with these feelings of displacement?

Well, I thought, I would write about the beauty around me, the nature on my doorstep. I would pay close attention; I would notice and capture the movements of birds; document the news brought in on the tide at the shoreline in front of the house, in the form of flotsam and jetsam, strewments of seaweed and – yes – plastic waste; identify shells and the creatures that had lately inhabited them, stones and their geological composition. I would turn myself into a naturalist. Except...

Except, that I have neither the persistence nor the patience for it. There is in Orkney a community of nature watchers so much more experienced and devoted than I am, employed to chart migrations of birds, count the numbers of endangered species, spot cetaceans, trap stoats, rescue seals. Added to them, there are the enthusiastic amateurs, haunters of the pages of Facebook, eager to communicate about the pod of orca in Scapa Flow, the likelihood of a good aurora display above the standing stones at the Ring of Brodgar, the rare species of moth, wild flower, migrant bird blown off course; who rush with their binoculars and cameras to capture the sightings and post them online.

'Where were you when this party kicked off?' my sister prodded me on Facebook. A whole gang of killer whales had been spotted cavorting for hours in Scapa Flow. Film of them was all over social media. I missed them.

Then again, imagine my embarrassment when on the phone to a friend, I exclaimed, 'Oh, I see a school of whales in Houton Bay!' And a moment later realised I'd been looking at a flock of starlings perched on telegraph wires, strung across the field between me and the sea. The tricks the Orkney light plays on you, alternately shrinking and magnifying distances.

While I'm on embarrassments, one of the most acute came with the realisation that I had attributed the breeding call of the curlew to its cousin the whimbrel, for no better reason than I had never learned that the streamer of light and sound trailing across the summer skies of my childhood belonged to the broon whaap; that the onomatopoeia of 'whimbrel' didn't entitle it to the song.

Worse still, I once heard a starling imitate the curlew call as you would hear it over fields in the distance and confidently told a well-known poet and nature writer that the impersonator was channelling a whimbrel.

But knowing the facts doesn't replace the magic of that music cascading from above on blue and green Orkney summer days. There is something about the *not* knowing that had its own enchantment, accompanying lost hours lying daydreaming in long grass at my grandparents' farm.

Walking back from there, from Viewfield in the country, when the nights were drawing in, to our house in Kirkwall, the whole family, eight of us, strung across the road, my father would sometimes say, watch out for the Merry Dancers. We watched but never saw them.

When, as an eighteen-year-old, I finally did see the Aurora Borealis, it was heart-stopping. The whole sky shimmered with a pale green, diaphanous curtain, rippling in an unfelt breeze. It appeared without warning in front of us as we drove to Evie. We stopped and got out. The cold and the ghostly curtain from another world seemed one. It lasted only moments then faded.

Since I came home I haven't been so lucky. Our house is to the south, with the Orphir hills north and west of us. The dancers rarely dance above our heads. One cold evening I drove all the way to Birsay when the Aurora Watchers were raving about the quality of the display. By the time I got there, the show was over. I drove home in the deep dark to pore over the – filtered – garish greens and pinks in the Facebook posts.

Truth to tell, I have sometimes found myself at odds with the nature-watching fraternity, alienated from the 'New Nature Writing'. A year home, I was visited one evening by a cat and her three kittens. I had seen her in that year, running up and down the road with voles and fieldmice in her mouth to feed three separate litters of kittens. She 'belonged', though she was an outside cat, still feral, to Elsie who had recently died. When she turned up, lying a few feet from my back door, with her latest batch of kittens, and looked me straight in the eye, I felt chosen. I gave them names: Ellie, the mother, Polly, Billie and Stevie.

There followed the involvement of Orkney Cats, trapping mother and kittens, driving them, yowling, to the vet to be neutered, feeding them outside, installing a cat flap and beds for them in the shed. Meanwhile, over on social media, the twitchers frequently inveighed against cat owners, deplored the deadly menace of the 'little old cat lady' facilitating the depletion of the stocks of Orkney vole, designed, apparently, only as food for raptors. No one, it seems, cares about the Orkney vole for its own sake.

But here was an interesting scenario. We often see hen harriers flying overhead, quartering the fields around, looking for prey. One day I watched a silver-grey male plunge from the sky, snatch a starling from the branches of the tree across the road, veer off and fly away. That was remarkable enough. But the kill triggered some atavistic knowledge in Stevie the cat, lying on the deck in front of the house. He leapt up, raced across the road, and plucked a shrew out of the grass from under the recent flight path of the hen harrier. The two events must have been related, though it's unclear how. There is no way even a cat's ears could have heard the shrew from that distance.

In my seven years home, I have witnessed one other remarkable raptor kill. I happened to glance out of the window to see a sparrowhawk dive into a flock of skeldros, capture one and repair to the hill. There it sat and performed its victory ceremony, plucking the feathers from its prey and tossing them, a miniature snowstorm, into the wind. While it did this, the other oystercatchers flew down in unison in great swoops over the head of the raptor. They kept this up for several minutes, before flying off. I fancied the flock was not prepared to abandon its captured member until all signs of life were gone. Or were they trying to threaten the sparrowhawk and scare it off through strength of numbers? Who knows? A better twitcher than I am, no doubt.

A few words in defence of the decision to take on Elsie's cats. From the moment their food is out, a procession of creatures comes for it. First the starlings, as soon as they hear the curtains open, line up on the guttering above the window with Hitchcockian burblings, taking their chances, between cats, to swoop down and grab some pellets. For two years running, a herring gull with a lump on its head, gave me the side eye through the window as it glided past to the dish for an easy meal.

The blackbirds are more standoffish. But last year, I watched a male on the deck feed two of its fledglings with the cats' food. Over several minutes he busied himself between the dish and the two youngsters, hopping over to feed each in turn, before filling his own beak and flying his unsteady offspring back to the nest. You would think I didn't put out fat balls and birdseed and mealy worms in feeders round the back. It seems they all prefer cat food pellets. If at night I forget to bring the dish in, I find in the morning, a silver tracery of slug and snail trails in and over and around it.

But what of beachcombing? The sea on my doorstep? My favourite way of losing myself in a reverie is to wander along the shore, looking at the variety of stones and shells, pocketing the odd one here and there, picking up sea glass and shards of sea-smoothed china.

Of another favourite pastime, hunting for groatie buckies, the tiny white and pink cowrie shells, *Cypraea Europaea*, I have grown weary. Or rather, jaded. There are popular spots for them in Orkney and I've noticed, as I step through the ebb, trying to get my eye in, that an unseemly competitiveness overtakes me and I resent the other stooped hunters on the sand. A recent search drew a blank and a wry comment from a fellow seeker who said, 'This beach has been strip-mined'. One day at the shore in Birsay, close to the start of the causeway over to the Brough, I stood at the edge of the water as the incoming tide deposited a dozen groatie buckies at my feet. Not satisfied with this unlooked for bounty, I trawled the shoreline for another hour, long past cold, greedy for more.

The first law of beachcombing: be thankful for what comes your way, unbidden.

But it seems I must learn this lesson over and over. I confess I'm not free of the tendencies I criticise in other nature watchers. There is a sight I would love to capture in words and images. It is when, in certain lights, a flock of skeldros takes flight from a field. On some days, phone camera set to video, I've shouted to scare them into the air, banged the metal bars of a farm gate, clapped my hands. It has never worked. The resulting films have not caught the flight. And what can words do?

Skeldros rise, dark smoke, turn as one, catch the light with forty flashes of silver, veer away.

'Carve the runes, then be content with silence', George Mackay Brown said.

Note to self: let go of the striving after spectacular sights, the thrill-seeking, the greed. Be content with those moments in the natural world, freely given. Even with no runes carved.

George Mackay Brown – A Portrait

Alexander Moffat

> 'A certain street in Edinburgh, Rose Street, I had heard
> about many a time.
> Once, they said, there had been forty pubs in that long
> dingy chasm; now they had shrunk to fourteen. And there
> prostitutes came out at night, like moths.'
>
> George Mackay Brown, *For The Islands I Sing*
> (John Murray, 1997)

While a young art student in the early 1960s, I haunted the
Rose Street bars with my closest friends, John Bellany and
Alan Bold, eager to participate in the thriving bohemian life
where poets, painters, jazz musicians, actors, publishers,
lawyers, politicians and students would congregate nightly.
There were pubs galore and if nothing much was happening in
one of them, a short walk to the next would plunge us into the
main action of the evening. As for the prostitutes (including
amongst their numbers shopgirls living above Jenners
Department Store in barrack-like conditions, desperate to
supplement their meagre wages) their presence lingered on in
the folklore of Rose Street, but they were no longer in business
and had long since disappeared. The poets were the main
attraction – Hugh MacDiarmid, Norman MacCaig, Sydney
Goodsir Smith, Tom Scott, George Campbell Hay and George
Mackay Brown were regulars and as far as we were concerned
something had happened in Scottish poetry that hadn't in
painting. We needed to keep company with such people. Not
everyone agreed, however, with Edwin Muir quipping that the

Milne's Bar drinkers were 'men of sorrows, afflicted by Grieve', but Milne's was also visited by Sean O'Casey, Dylan Thomas, the Indian poet Dom Moraes and T S Eliot amongst others. To begin with John Bellany and I kept our distance; we were painters, not aspiring writers, but thanks to Alan Bold, we gradually became known and were able to exchange a few words with our heroes. I was fortunate in having a girlfriend who as a student teacher was placed in the school where Norman MacCaig was Headmaster and we soon found ourselves invited to parties in his house after closing time on Saturday nights. This led to a friendship with Norman that survived until the end of his days.

There was nothing refined or respectable about Edinburgh's bohemia. In his *Memoirs of a Modern Scotland*, Karl Miler says, 'It bred this tradition of conviviality and talk. The passion in the Rose Street pubs had to be heard to be believed'. The Orcadian poet George Mackay Brown usually had a word or two to say to us; we were fellow students after all – he was a postgraduate student at Edinburgh University involved in a study of Gerard Manley Hopkins, the poet and Jesuit priest. A solitary figure, George often appeared on the fringe of conversations with his fellow poets. He did, however, enjoy a special friendship with Stella Cartwright, one of the few women who braved the basement environment of Milne's. It seems when they first met she thought he was a fisherman. George was deeply attracted to Stella, sending a poem on her birthday up until her death in 1985. As an observer of the Rose Street spectacle one of my enduring memories is of George in his trademark camel coloured duffle coat tumbling to the floor from a high stool at the bar in the Abbotsford, picking himself up and finishing off his pint of beer. Let's be clear, he wasn't the only one in an inebriated state on a Friday night. George unsparingly describes similar drinking sessions in his memoir *For the Islands I Sing*: 'There were a few sore heads and guilt-hauntings, after particularly severe sessions; but, looking back, it was a time of delight and laughter'. Such was the boisterousness and fun of those days and nights that the more serious and lasting experiences gained might easily be overlooked. This was a time when we tasted life and art and literature to the full, a crucial moment in the long journey we knew would be necessary in order to become an artist. There was no question of painting portraits of the poets at this stage – that would come later, once I felt properly equipped and ready to take on something truly ambitious.

In the summer of 1967, again with John Bellany and Alan Bold, I made my first visit to Germany, both East and West, coming face to face with the works of the great painters of the Weimar Republic. In their incisive and penetrating images of modern life, Beckmann, Dix and Grosz showed that the modern portrait was capable of a direct engagement with humanity and fired up by the impact of their work, I launched into a new phase of portrait painting. At the beginning of 1968, I made portraits of Bellany and Bold, with the novelist Archie Hind and Norman MacCaig following in quick succession. Eager to pursue a literary theme I approached George one evening in Milne's and asked if he might like to come to the studio and sit for me. He readily agreed and an afternoon date was arranged, but when it came to the day he failed to appear and not long after returned to Orkney and that seemed to be that!

A decade later, in early 1978, I received a letter from the Scottish Arts Council advising me of a scheme entitled 'Art for

Public Places'. In my reply I said I didn't have any plans for a large mural, but instead, made an alternative proposal to paint individual portraits of the generation of Scottish poets from Hugh MacDiarmid onwards, the poets of the Scottish Renaissance – Sorley MacLean, Norman MacCaig, Robert Garioch, Edwin Morgan, Iain Crichton Smith and George Mackay Brown. The 'public' aspect of the project would see the completed portraits installed in galleries/museums close to the 'homelands' of each of the poets. In that sense the portraits were conceived as public paintings, to be viewed in public spaces. There was a positive response from the Scottish Arts Council and 'The Seven Poets' commission as it was called, took me all over Scotland, from the Borders to the Hebrides and up to Orkney. With every one of the poets I intended to portray, it's the specific sense of place, the locality and terrain that informs and nourishes their vision. Without setting foot in their territory there could be no proper understanding of their work. At long last, I would travel to Orkney to paint George and this time there would be no distractions.

I arrived in Stromness at the beginning of April 1980. On my way to George's little council house at Mayburn Court I was struck by the uniqueness of the place, the buildings, the narrow main street paved with flagstones, the wee lanes, the little piers and slipways, altogether unlike any other town in Scotland. Here I was, in Hamnavoe. We got down to work right away with George a willing participant, sitting in his rocking chair, surrounded by books on shelves and on tables and chairs and in large cardboard boxes on the floor. It seems to me all successful portraits are collaborations – the sitter prepares himself or herself for the event and the artist responds. Without this kind of human interaction painting a portrait would merely be a technical exercise. I was later to discover George had received a letter from Robert Garioch (whose portrait I had already completed) assuring him there was nothing to fear in sitting for his portrait. When I started drawing I could see the tuberculosis he was diagnosed with as a young man had left its mark. His reclusive life would also have to be taken into account and all of this would somehow or other have to find its way into the finished portrait.

L-R: NORMAN MACCAIG, GEORGE MACKAY BROWN AND ALEXANDER MOFFAT IN ORKNEY, 1981
(COURTESY ALEXANDER MOFFAT)

George was keen to hear news of his fellow poets and I was able to tell him about my recent encounters with MacDiarmid, Garioch, MacCaig and Edwin Morgan and also about my visits to Ian Hamilton Finlay, who had briefly lived on Rousay and had encouraged George to send his poems and short stories to the *Glasgow Herald*. The era of the Rose Street poets ended when Bob Watt, the legendary manager of Milne's, retired at the end of the 1960s and there was nothing much to report on that front, but there were countless tales to be re-told of those wild times and a host of shared memories to pore over and dissect. I mentioned I was thinking about a painting of the poets together, placing them in a space that would borrow features from Milne's, The Abbotsford and The Cafe Royal. George was enthusiastic: 'My, that's a wonderful painting you have in mind'. From that moment on, I knew I would have to tackle a big group portrait and with Sydney Goodsir Smith's *Kind Kittock's Land* providing essential source material, I started work on a large painting, now known as 'Poets' Pub'.

> 'Grieve and Garioch aye tuim their pints...
> While lean MacCaig stains sniffing the western seas
> And Brown leads wi his Viking chin...'

After an hour or so George would go into the kitchen and brew up his brand of strong tea, as black as a pint of Guinness, but not nearly as pleasant. Fortunately, there was a plentiful supply of chocolate biscuits to temper the bitter taste of the tea. There was home brew on the menu as well, but I treated that with an extra degree of caution. We worked this way for three or four days until my sketchbooks were full – head and hand studies, drawings and pastels of the furniture and living room, as well as landscapes and harbour views – and I was satisfied I had more than enough information to begin the portrait proper. We would pause when the postman arrived with the morning mail. Invitations to take part in prestigious poetry festivals in the USA, Australia and Canada were opened and shuffled aside. 'Why would I want to go to these far away places?' was his final word on the matter. For George everything was on Orkney. He saw the small community as a microcosm with the whole world gathered around him in Stromness itself. He was a storyteller who stayed at home, intimately connected to the locality, to the characters and histories of the place. In his poems the daily rituals of ordinary life appear alongside references to the great Norse sagas and the threat of uranium mining in Yesnaby. In George's writings history and modernity sit side by side.

I had booked into the Stromness Hotel thinking I would see George there in the evenings, only to discover he was no longer welcome on the premises. I never found out precisely why, but presumed he must have been 'carried away' one evening. Like all poets and artists, he enjoyed a drink, but knew where it might lead – his reference to a whisky bottle as 'the smiler with the knife' speaks volumes. Being banned from the Stromness Hotel, however, turned out a blessing in disguise as George transferred his allegiance to the Braes Hotel. As the name suggests, The Braes was situated half way up Brinkie's Brae and had a little conservatory attached with magnificent views looking across and beyond to Scapa Flow in the far distance. This was now George's favoured bar and would eventually provide the setting for the finished portrait. I say eventually, as my first thoughts placed George at home in his rocking chair within a vertical composition, his duffle coat hanging on the back of a door and a view to the harbour from a window.

I worked on this first version for a month or so, but became dissatisfied with the result. Rather than flog a dead horse I made a fresh start on a new canvas. Painting is neither a straight-forward nor a predetermined process. On re-examining my initial sketches it became clear the Braes Hotel setting had everything I was looking for in terms of the poet and his place – it would allow me to develop in the seascape and landscape a more definitive view of Orkney, of the farming, fishing and seafaring communities that had inhabited those islands for centuries. John Berger's description of landscape and what he calls the 'address' of a place is important in this context. Berger writes that paintable landscapes are those in which what is visible 'enhances man'. In any landscape 'mood' may change but the 'address of the landscape' does not change. The address of the islands of Scotland is tidal and recurring, ancient yet contemporary. George always maintained a wonderfully rich relationship with the landscape/seascape of

ALEXANDER MOFFAT RESTORING HIS PORTRAIT OF GEORGE MACKAY BROWN
(COURTESY ALEXANDER MOFFAT)

Orkney and as soon as I started on the new canvas the portrait literally painted itself.

The portrait was first displayed in Orkney as part of the 'Seven Poets' exhibition at Pier Arts Centre in Stromness during the St Magnus Festival in 1981. Thereafter it was transferred from the Scottish Arts Council Collection to Orkney Museums and hung for many years in Stromness Academy. When the portrait was sent to the Lillie Art Gallery in 2018 to take its place in the exhibition 'Landmarks', alongside the other six portraits and 'Poets' Pub', brought together for the first time since the original 'Seven Poets' exhibition, it was discovered that the surface of the painting had been badly damaged by rainwater. My offer to carry out the necessary repair work was accepted and this was completed later in 2018, and the portrait returned to Orkney, where it now hangs in the Tankerness Museum in Kirkwall.

Restoring a painting made 40 years previously isn't something I've done on a regular basis. When confronted with a youthful work, the temptation is to repaint the whole thing, to make a fresh start and create anew – always a risky business as there is no guarantee against it all going wrong. In this case that was never an option as I was acutely aware my task was to repair, not repaint the portrait. By a stroke of good fortune, George's head and hands were relatively undamaged and there was no need for any kind of drastic intervention on those areas of the portrait. It was simply a case of removing the watermarks and stains and renewing the faded colour. Renovating the damaged portrait was a labour of love, just as painting the portrait was in the first place.

Filming *The Storm Watchers* During Covid

Gerda Stevenson

Just over two years ago, I landed in Orkney during a storm. I was coming to Stromness to give the George Mackay Brown Memorial lecture, on the subject of Margaret Tait, as part of her centenary celebrations. The plane had banked at an alarming angle as it approached Kirkwall's runway – that's how you land a plane in a storm I was told. The taxi's windscreen wipers ploughed through troughs of rain all the way from Kirkwall to Stromness. From my eyrie at the top of the Ferry Inn, I saw huge waves slapping Stromness pier, the lampposts wagging like plastic straws. I was a storm watcher. I had no inkling then that another kind of tempest would soon be sweeping the whole world.

During the second lockdown, I received a call from composer Alasdair Nicolson, director of Orkney's St Magnus International Festival. Would I be interested in directing an open-air community theatre production of George Mackay Brown's play *The Storm Watchers* for the 2021 festival? The cast was to be made up of local people. My mind was racing with delight – I love George's writing. I met him on several occasions through mutual friends Gunnie Moberg and the artist and publisher Simon Fraser. One of the greatest pleasures of my professional life has been directing community theatre. Through my work as a writer and actor, I've visited Orkney many times and the fiercest trowies can't keep me away. Interested? I'm on board! The only snag was that the production might not actually happen: we were in the eye of a pandemic storm.

At that point no-one knew when Covid restrictions might be lifted. As I write this, we're still unsure as to what may or may not be possible regarding large gatherings of people attending a live performance in Scotland, even out of doors. So the fall-back position was that we could make a film of the play instead, to be screened over the internet. It soon became clear that this was the most viable option, and that I would have to direct the film online. And so, I've spent most days during the last two months visiting Orkney virtually, from my bedroom via Zoom.

The Storm Watchers was first published in 1967, in Mackay Brown's superb short story collection *A Calendar of Love.* He subtitles *The Storm Watchers* as 'a play for voices'. It's a unique piece of writing, because without requiring adaptation, it lends itself readily to different dramatic forms – radio, stage and screen. Timeless and archetypal, the story of seven women whose men drown at sea one stormy night, this play is an Orcadian sister to Synge's *Riders to the Sea* and Donald Campbell's *The Widows of Clyth.* Like all Mackay Brown's writing, the language is poetic, heightened and breathtakingly concise: 'The night was dark, a shut oyster.' 'Stars swarmed across my bride window like sillocks.' And there's that hallmark ritualistic, incantatory style to the writing, with repetition of particular lines throughout.

Mackay Brown frequently refers to hands in this play – hands joined together in marriage, hands squeezing fish oil into lamps, hands net-mending – so, so many hands:

'On account of James, my brother, I have sour, chaste hands.'

'My father put an oar in Ally's hand.'

'One night my father put our hands together, Tors with Ruth.'

'And a summer day, he filled my white hands with cod's liver.'

'The way he would turn a bit of tarry twine upon itself with his witty fingers, and knot it...'

There's something deeply human and vulnerable about this part of our anatomy and all its associated activity – hard labour, love, exchange, abuse – so closely observed by Mackay Brown. I decided to use hands as a recurring visual *motif*.

There's nothing sentimental about the text – domestic abuse and hypocrisy are deftly hinted at. One of the fishermen's widows says of her kirk elder husband: 'Before a year was out I had more kicks than kisses from him...' And there's also a thread of racism – another widow says of her beloved: 'They brought him from the tooth of the sea, a peedie, black, sodden man. They filled his foreign throat with whisky...the children would run in terror from his foreign face; the fishermen were surly at him...' Fascinating to consider that during the 60s, at the height of Apartheid in South Africa, Mackay Brown was writing about racism in Orkney.

Since its publication, the play has been taken up by many theatre groups, amateur and professional. In order to meet with the stipulated minimum length for plays submitted to the Scottish Community Drama Association, Mackay Brown added three spoken choral voice sections to the original text. These are very theatrical in style, requiring carefully synchronised choral speaking, and don't lend themselves so easily to film the way the original play does – a good deal of adaptation would be required to make them work smoothly for screen. I've been tussling with this, and have incorporated only the first of these additional choral sections, having found a way of weaving the words and images into the body of the original text as it appears in *A Calendar of Love*.

The play is structured as a series of monologues delivered by seven women, interspersed with single lines uttered in a communal voice. This offers an ideal form under the restrictions of lockdown: each woman is – at least psychologically – separate and alone, although part of a group, described in the scene-setting by Mackay Brown: *A long shore. Darkness. Seven women standing.*

So we had two approaches to the process of filming. The first, to have each woman film her own monologues on her smartphone in her home; and the second (once restrictions allowed), employ a professional cameraman to film the footage of all the women standing on the shore, socially distanced.

We began with the interiors. I felt like something of an invader, entering people's houses on Zoom, asking the cast members to take me round their homes on their smartphones, choosing locations that would suit each character. I found myself brazenly asking: 'Could you shift that bookshelf?' 'Can you switch the fridge off? It's making a dreadful hum!' 'Could we have a look through your wardrobe to see what you might have that's suitable to wear?' Luckily, every single cast member has been completely committed to the unusual circumstances and demands of this extraordinary process. There was only a slight frisson at one point when I asked if a curtain might be removed and was told, 'My auntie might not be too keen'.

As soon as we had the go-ahead, the cast (Cally Bevan, Vera Butler, Eleanor Dean, Lorraine Giles, Phyllis McLaughlin,

Iona McLeod, Ruth McTaggart, Dawn Norquoy, Jane Partridge and Holly Sonabend) immediately started WhatsApping one another about costume availability. A couple of them looked through the stores of local drama clubs. But we used only a very few items from there – I decided that I wanted to avoid a quaint Victorian bonnets and skirts look, preferring to give the film a timeless feel, deliberately mixing things up. After discussion with our editor, we chose to present the film in black and white, which itself immediately creates an illusion of times past. To find a way of incorporating the first of Mackay Brown's 'choral voice' sections, I searched through Orkney Library's archive of old photos of women working on the land, ploughing and harvesting. These we've presented in colour, as a contrast to the rest of the film, which, like the story itself, is stark and austere.

Extreme patience and trust were essential on everyone's part, working through this slow process of filming. Most of the actors have worked only in amateur theatre before, and never on film, so it took time to find the right level of performance. So much was being demanded of them – trying to capture the exact framing I had in mind, setting up their smartphones on the tripod, fixing the focus, struggling with the microphone, getting the lighting right, with no professional technical people around to help. The framing was never quite the same as it was on Zoom, but we got used to compensating for this. Then, having rehearsed, and achieved what we wanted, I'd wave goodbye, and wait for the actor to film herself. Then she'd send the result online for me to download, look at and make notes. More often than not, we'd get back onto Zoom, re-rehearse, and do it all again. So much slower than if we'd been in the same room, and I'd been able to watch each take as it happened.

Meantime, there were many 'cutaway' shots I needed. I had 'satellite crews' – individuals filming additional necessary footage in Orkney, Glasgow and also here in my own Scottish Borders neighbourhood, where I'd be shamelessly phoning up my godson: 'Sean – could you come round with your dad, and bring your camera and a spade? I need to film some grave-digging!'

A few days later, Sean's father, Mackay Brown's old friend Simon Fraser, was spotted digging a grave in the field next to my house, much to the consternation of passers-by. Sean had all the angles shot and Simon filled in 'the grave', the field restored to green normality in no time.

'Sean – can you come round and film washing blowing on the line? And any chance of filming stars swarming like sillocks?'

'Stars swarming like *what*?!'

'Like fish – they're pollock, saithe – you know, coalfish.'

'Well, I could try filming stars on a time-lapse...'

'Great! Oh, and could you also do my hand putting a vase of lupins in the window?'

We both wore masks, and kept the kitchen door wide open for maximum exchange of air as I placed the vase of flowers on the windowsill.

Lupins. Mackay Brown seems to have loved them. They are a recurring motif in *A Calendar of Love*, lupins in fields and gardens, picked and placed in vases, and *The Lupin* – a boat of that name. I love this flower too – my mother used to grow hosts of them in her garden when I was a child, and their multi-coloured spires soared in my imagination. Unfortunately, winter isn't the season for these blooms, but I wanted that moment to be in the film – a little signal, a homage to George – so I searched online, and found a store that sold silk versions that looked surprisingly realistic. I won't forget the thrill I felt when those three silk lupins arrived in their long cardboard box, exquisitely wrapped in tissue paper, looking as lovely and serviceable as I'd hoped.

Meanwhile, professional cameraman Fionn McArthur, and Mike Partridge, who'd been helping out with additional footage, had been out on a rainy night in Stromness with a small number of the cast (fewer than the maximum allowed to gather outside under Covid restrictions). Fionn and Mike were filming them running through the streets and knocking urgently on doors. The police happened to be out at the same time, and our *Storm Watchers* team assumed they were checking that Covid rules were being adhered to. In fact, the police were visiting a household whose door a cast member was knocking on – pre-arranged with that family. Confusion and hilarity arose when the police chapped the same door, and the family didn't respond – they'd been given instructions by our team *not* to open the door when they heard the knocking!

Eventually, we'd completed filming all the interior monologues, and were now waiting for Covid restrictions to be eased so that we could shoot the women standing on the shore, watching the storm in vain hope of their men's safe return. By the time it was possible, the ideal stormy weather had passed. The first night proved to be a flat calm, so filming was cancelled. I started to fear we might lose the cast – with Covid restrictions easing, people would understandably wish to travel, if at all possible. This production was a community venture, with an amateur cast. We were relying on their goodwill. Throughout the whole period of filming, I had to make myself available for directing on Zoom whenever it fitted into their schedule – most of them had jobs. One of the actors had booked to take the ferry from Stromness the day before the rescheduled filming, so an extra night-shoot had to be arranged before she left. Again, a flat calm. So a leaf-blower was requisitioned by Charlotte Rendall of the St Magnus Festival. She and her husband gave it a trial run in their back garden before taking it down to the shore, and thus the wind was manufactured! On the second night, when the full cast was present, not only did the flat calm prevail, but a Second World War grenade had been discovered in the locality, and all roads in and out of Stromness were closed. Eventually the team got themselves down to Warbeth beach, with storm lanterns and leaf-blower. Fionn managed to film the stunningly atmospheric shots of the women we needed. All the while, I'd been scratching about at home here in the Borders, like a mother hen without her chicks, having sent my shot list to Fionn, along with detailed directorial instructions to the cast, wondering how it was all going.

As I write, I'm now working on the final edit, with composer Alasdair Nicolson, who, as director of the St Magnus International Festival, instigated the whole project, editor James Alcock and sound designer Rob MacNeacail.

At times, I've felt I've been navigating through a storm of changeable circumstances, but throughout this extraordinary production there has been only goodwill from everyone involved. At the front of our communal mind has been our debt to George. A deeply fulfilling community venture, beautifully captured in this moving poem, by Vera Butler, who works as a carer. One of *The Storm Watchers* cast, who has recently turned to writing, Vera sent me her poem yesterday, at the end of filming, a tribute to our project, and to George (featured opposite).

The Resting Place

by Vera Butler

No one did I ken in that kirkyard –
they stood aloof in thir weel tended lairs,
a place o comfort for many
but not for me.

We met beside the kirkyard wall,
some folk I kent, some unkan tae me,
walking the road tae the shore,
a distance between us no only in feet,
my accent broadest of aall.

The shore when reached ower gress and stones
wis a place o beauty and serenity in this mad world,
the Hoy hills so near I could almost reach oot and touch thim.
Comfortingly close tonight.

The film crew – weel a slight exaggeration! –
guided us throo the movements,
and laughter and sadness mingled
beside the cowld blue, black sea.
Fingers numbing wae the sinking sun.

Oil lamps and torches noo lit for the final shots,
a feeling of bonding taegither tae dae wir best.
Wid George feel this love o his wark vibrate
throo rock, gress and earth tae his eternal bed?
Or wis he here wae is?

So here I stood on Warbeth shore as Kittag,
waiting and hoping beside the dark sea
that my man Peter would be washed ashore
and I would find him dead,
dead like my feelings for him.
Only then could my life start again,
without fear and toil and sadness.

Hid felt that night like we stepped back in time
something so timeless in a wey,
the power o the sea, the hills o Hoy darkening
and looming bigger the darker it got.
The rhythm o the waves broken only by the caall
o the eider ducks silhouetted
against the dying light in the west
as they cam home tae roost.

And there we stood reluctant tae leave
till the cowld made is shift.
Torches and lamps lit wir path
and voices and accents mingled taegither
as we cam tae the kirkyard waall, and whar
before I thowt I kent no one,
I stopped and whispered thank you
tae a man I'd nivver met.

The Wind that Shakes the Islands

Kenny Taylor

There's a warm breeze, suffused with salt and seaweed, blowing in from the ocean. A few hundred metres away, a line of white water in the channel between the island and the Orkney mainland roars where currents clash. Everywhere else on sea and land is quiet as I look around from the top of a stairway to nowhere.

There are eight steps in all, then nothing. Just a void between the curve of steps, the wall of an old grey building and some lower structures, all roofless. A fulmar glides past; another cackles; the soft wind carries seal calls, then snatches them away.

> Crossed hands, scent of holy water...
> The storm danced over all that night
>> Loud with demons, but I
>> Safe in Brother Colm's cell.
>
> Next morning in tranced sunshine
> The corn lay squashed on every hill;
>> Tang and tern were strewn
>> Among high pastures.
>
> I tell you this, my son; after
> That Godsent storm, I find peace here
>> These many years with
>> The Gray Monks of Eynhallow.[1]

---

1 George Mackay Brown, 'The Storm' in Archie Bevan and Brian Murray (eds), *The Collected Poems of George Mackay Brown* (2005), p.4.

I don't know if George Mackay Brown ever got ashore on the hallowed isle that features in 'The Storm', published in his debut collection nearly 70 years ago. It can be a tricky place to reach, as I found some years ago, when I joined a small group of seabird researchers from the University of Aberdeen on one of their summer visits to study fulmars there. By coincidence, that work began around the time that George was making his first forays into print.

Descending the low stair, I push through lush buttercups and nettles to enter the church porch and nave. The oldest Romanesque stonework here could date from the 1100s, when there may have been some kind of religious establishment on Eynhallow; when the Vikings held sway over the Orkney archipelago; when Magnus voyaged and returned and prayed and was butchered on neighbouring Egilsay. No one is sure.

Except George. In the clarity of his images, the power of his invocations of blasts and blessings, storm-blown tide wrack and 'tranced' sunshine, he is sure and confident. He sees the monks, feels a tranquillity in the lines he shapes and the symbols he finds while thinking of this place – a place he may never have known in detail.

So often, those are elements of why I'm drawn to his poetry and short prose down the years. For although it's commonplace for him to be considered a writer who somehow defines key aspects of Orkney life and scenes, very often that's not what I draw from his work. This echoes some aspects of an essay I co-wrote not long ago with Duncan MacLean, who lives and works on mainland Orkney, where we discussed 'North' as a concept and Duncan said:

...tourists are attracted to places by fictional animals like Nessie, and fictionalized versions of real people like Mary Queen of Scots, and fictional locations from *Outlander*. But what attracts and excites you and me is just as fictional: the notion that 'North' is something more than a relative geographical description: the idea that George Mackay Brown's fantasies describe an Orkney that ever really existed; the wish-fulfilment that Sigrid Undset's politics represent the politics of far-northerners better than Knut Hamsun's.[2]

Or as Robert Crawford said:

Brown's digging-in led him to write about an Orkney that would never exist, one that only the dewy-eyed (or those over-eager for tourist dollars) could construe as a real place. There is a tendency of this kind even in his best work.[3]

These days, published work by George is stocked in abundance in the bookshops of Stromness and Kirkwall. It's a boon for Orcadians and visitors alike to have such a range of his writing available in fresh editions, ranged from floor to ceiling. I wonder what readers new to him and new to Orkney might expect to find, and relish the thought that many will be surprised, not by descriptions of the Orkney scene, but by unexpected ideas and by the rhythms of seedtime, growth, harvest, death and eternity that rock beneath the apparent simplicity of his lines.

---

2   Duncan MacLean and Kenny Taylor, 'The Flicker of North' in Gail Low and Kirsty Gunn (eds), *Imagined Spaces* (2020), p.127.

3   Robert Crawford, 'In Bloody Orkney', *London Review of Books*, 29:4 (2007).

That he could make those lines sing in both poetry and prose was acknowledged early on by people like his friend and mentor, Edwin Muir – and before that by the un-named teacher who repeatedly gave him top marks for school essays. Many others, including Seamus Heaney, echoed that appreciation over the following decades. Considering prose, Alan Bold, wrote in 1978:

> George Mackay Brown's greatest achievement, in my opinion, is to be found in his ability as a storyteller.
> It is a gift, a remarkable ability, and he is unique in his matter and manner (though he has learned from the writing of Thomas Mann, E M Forster, Jorge Luis Borges).[4]

For poetry, Gerard Manley Hopkins, perhaps pre-eminently, could be added to the list of literary greats who influenced him. Writing after visiting a Hopkins exhibition in Oxford in the centenary of the poet's death, George said of him that:

> In his life he was never in Orkney, but one can feel his spirit here too, in the rapture of a skylark singing, in the cold clean thrilling wash of the sea against Yesnaby and Birsay, in the midsummer rush and cluster of the wild flowers with the morning dew about them; and in the fish and animals and folk, every one distinct and unique, a never-to-be-repeated joy.[5]

---

4 Alan Bold, *George Mackay Brown* (1978), p.50.

5 Quoted in Alan Riach, *Gerald Manley Hopkins and Scotland*, Gerald Manley Hopkins Society lecture (2008).

In the centenary of the Orkney writer's birth, those words seem to say as much about him as they do about Hopkins – acknowledging a shared perception of what energises their work. 'The force that through the green fuse drives the flower', is there, to quote another poet who influenced George's early work, but so too is a sense of something more, perhaps linked to the cycles that permeate so much of his writing.

In both poetry and prose, aspects of which I value in equal measure, narrative power glows within the often few words or short sentences. I can never tire of 'Beachcomber', where every stanza suggests a story beyond it, then moves to another idea, retrieved from the tide rim and the flow of time in a procession through the seven days (a number that fascinated him) in the week:

> Wednesday a half can of Swedish spirits
> I tilted my head.
> The shore was cold with mermaids and angels.[6]

Or in the elegy, 'Hamnavoe', imagining Stromness seen by his postman father as he moves through the small town:

> A tinker keened like a tartan gull
> At cuithe-hung doors. A crofter lass
> > Trudged through the lavish dung
> > In a dream of cornstalks and milk.[7]

The pleasure in lines like these doesn't fade with repeated reading, nor – for me – do often-repeated references to similar objects, crops, food, weather and types of people. Butter and honeycombs, hawk and harvest, new-baked loaves, nets and

6 Brown, 'Beachcomber' in *Collected Poems,* p.123.
7 Brown, 'Hamnavoe' in *Collected Poems,* p.24.

ploughs, ministers and spinsters and saints and martyrs, tinkers, ale, barleycorn and fiddlers. I could add many more. And through it all, the relishing of Viking-era names and Norse words that have weathered the centuries since their first use on the islands, especially in the naming of Orkney places. 'The names of the old farms are functional, powerful, beautiful –' he wrote, 'Skaill, Queryostray, Lyking, Stymilders, Breckness, Corse, Tormiston'.[8]

For me, George mines his knowledge of Orkney, both through his life in Stromness and his liking for some periods in Orkney history, to find ore from which to mould the symbols that glint through the narratives of both prose and poems. He doesn't describe Orkney in ways that some others might if writing about its landscapes and seascapes, nature and local people. There are larks in abundance in his work, for example, but I don't look to him for anything in the way of 'nature writing'. There are tales of individuals and communities that draw me in, but I make little use of them as sources of Orcadian history. Away from the poems and prose pieces (including local newspaper columns) set in Stromness and Rackwick, George doesn't transport me to many other parts of the isles. Some of that could be because he didn't travel much, even within his own small archipelago. In many ways, he didn't need to.

When I visit different Orkney islands, from North Ronaldsay and Papay to South Walls, West Mainland to Deerness, Sule Skerry to Copinsay, as I have done through many years, I can hold some of George's words in mind, yet not feel the need to relate them directly to what I'm seeing, who I'm meeting. Even on Eynhallow, or on Egilsay, the holy ground of St Magnus' martyrdom, he's partly there, largely not.

---

8 George Mackay Brown and Sylvia Wishart, *An Orkney Tapestry* (1973), p.22.

For I know that 'his' Orkney, both real and imagined, is one – or several – Orkneys that had faded before his lifetime. Much of his work is set in centuries previous to his own. This is most obvious in his fascination with the high period of Viking rule in the isles and with Magnus, but also in his tales of Orkney folk drawn from life in the eighteenth and nineteenth centuries – or earlier, in the case of the pirate, John Gow. Where the present impinges, it is often as a source of destructive influences.

I used to think of George's well-known dislike of 'progress' and modernity as a bit quaint. Now, at a time of human-driven climate crisis and loss of nature, I'm not so sure. Within 'An Orkney Tapestry', first published in 1969, the following passages gave me a jolt the other day:

> There is a new religion, Progress, in which we all devoutly believe, and it is concerned only with material things in the present and in a vague golden-handed future. It is a rootless utilitarian faith, without beauty or mystery...
> It is difficult to picture this goddess of plenty other than as some huge computer figure, that will give our children what they desire easily and endlessly – food, sex, excitement – a synthetic goddess, vast and bland as a Buddha, but without love or tenderness or compassion; activated only by a mania to create secondary objects that become increasingly shinier and shoddier and uglier.[9]

As the oceans choke with plastic, spewing rubbish onto Orkney shores, as everywhere, filling the guts of fish and fulmar alike; as instant gratification of consumer desires for objects,

9 Brown and Wishart, *Orkney Tapestry,* pp.20-1.

221

however useless, becomes the norm, his sentiments seem ever more relevant. Yet this was a writer whose life was likely saved – and much extended to write the bulk of his work – by the medical science that produced streptomycin. That was the subject of one of the world's first 'blind' clinical trials of a drug, was the first antibiotic effective against the TB that blighted him and which opened the way for new avenues of progress in clinical practice.

He did acknowledge the potential contradiction. When asked in 1980, in the 'Seven Poets' film project, whether there was 'anything positive to be said for progress', he replied that he wouldn't be here if it weren't for progress in medical science, which had also been a general benefit to others.[10] Perhaps I'm romanticising, but I tend to think of George's attitude to the everyday present and possible future as reflecting something of his fascination with what he saw as the rhythms of deeper time, linked to the brevity of human lives and to communities of distinctively different individuals.

The short BBC Scotland film, 'The Valley of the Sea', featuring George and his friend and collaborator, the composer Sir Peter Maxwell Davies, in Rackwick, is revelatory in this respect.[11] There are many pleasures in it, including being able to hear George's gentle, precise way of speaking. It's the composer who dives into the ocean of time in some of what he says:

> ...living in a place like Rackwick...one's life is governed by the rising and setting of the sun.
> And probably by the rising and setting of the moon,

---

10 Christopher Carrell (ed), *Seven Poets* (1981), p.55

11 Peter Maxwell Davies, in Howie Firth (prod and audio recording), *The Valley by the Sea*, BBC Radio Scotland (1982).

although you're not that aware of it because that relates to the tides, and even on a surface level, the tide's coming in and out relates to when you go down there to collect driftwood or not. You become very conscious of these natural rhythms. And also the much bigger cycle of natural rhythms to do with the spring and the summer and the winter. In fact, what George Mackay Brown so often talks about in his poetry: that your life becomes a ritual which is related to these large, perennial time cycles.

I only once glimpsed George. It was early on a winter's evening in the middle of Stromness. I was navigating the curves of meandering flagstones in the semi-darkness when a figure emerged from one of the steep side passages that link the town's hill buildings to Hamnavoe's core. Almost immediately, the jutting jawline and sweep of hair showed me that this was indeed George. I didn't think it appropriate to rush up and try to make conversation; to tell him how much I valued his writing. In any case, it was the briefest of sightings. So what I most remember is not any shared words (more's the pity), but noticing how, when he looked at the lit window of a nearby licensed grocer's as he turned to walk towards it, his face also lit with immediate pleasure, as if a cloud had shifted to reveal the sun.

His old friend, David Campbell, wrote of how – coming to attend the low-key launch of 'Letters to Gypsy' in George's Stromness council house the autumn of 1990 – he was greeted as usual by the 'shy, curly-haired, blue-eyed Orcadian, soft of speech, courteous, fond of a pint and company'.[12] And how

---

12 David Campbell, 'Carried along by rhythms of childhood', *The Scotsman*, 13 October 1990, p.13

George 'characteristically' welcomed him with 'a sudden, surprising smile'.

Although I only once caught a flash of that smile, the image stays. It roots the symbols and rhythms of his work in the very human warmth of a man who celebrated the richness of his home place, even as he stretched his imagination from Orkney to eternity and back again.

• • •

Even in wet overcast, the waters of the sounds around the big isle of Rousay keep a freshness of pale blue and green in them. Repeated journeys have made me fall ever more deeply under the spell of this part of Orkney. Today, my daughter, Alice, is with me, and Egilsay will add to that allure for both of us.

As the small ferry leaves Rousay and pushes northwards, gangs of long-tailed ducks are flocking in the aquamarine channels, plumes of spray lifting as they splash down. The island of Wyre, childhood home of Edwin Muir, sits smoored in grey mirk to the south-east. As the ferry nears the Egilsay pier, the tower of St Magnus Church is an unmistakable landmark.

The cult of St Magnus was massive in the north by the later twelfth century. But although his name would remain in use beyond the Middle Ages through the cathedral dedicated to him in Kirkwall, his fame faded over most of the last few centuries. That things changed in the later twentieth century is thanks in large measure to George's writing and his collaborations with Sir Peter Maxwell Davies. Together, they made Magnus once more the saint of choice when it comes to the Christian traditions of these lovely, windswept isles.

Crossing a field (where a ram is wheezing with some force) we reach the roofless church. Inside, details of its neat twelfth-century stonework seem little altered since the place was built, around 1117, to commemorate Magnus's death here. I think of the strangeness of Magnus – who almost willed his own martyrdom, according to the sagas – and to the legacy of saint and poet and composer: a trinity of lives that has helped to shape some of how present-day Orkney is viewed by so many people.

There's a sheen of rain on the stones of the tower. Within the funnel at its core, open to the sky, the wind whirls. It keeps a drone of breathy sound resonating and shifting, as if the whole, lofty structure has been raised to the lips of an unseen flautist. On first hearing, it sounds like the same note, but there's more, much more, when I really listen.

The Orkney wind that shakes crops and seas and sheep and tide wrack, that rattles the roof-tiles of Stromness and Rackwick, that touches fisherfolk and farmers and children alike, is alive among the old stones today. And through its weavings, the void sings.

My Uncle George

Ros Taylor

Many trees have been felled to produce the words written by and about my uncle, George Mackay Brown. He would have been 100 years old this year and, to mark this auspicious event, many more words will flow from the keyboards of literary giants across the globe. This pencil sketch of the man I knew as my uncle is no literary masterpiece, but a collection of fond memories recalled by me of a time during the 1950s and early 60s when George was a student in Edinburgh and, later, when he came visiting us.

My family was made up of Dad, Norrie (George's older brother), Mum, Hazel and two older sisters, Allison and Pamela. We had moved to Edinburgh from Orkney in 1954 in order for Dad to take up a teaching post as a teacher of English and History. I was four years old then and my sisters six and ten. Two years later, we finally settled in a brand new council house in a new housing estate called Oxgangs. In that modest little house we spent many happy years. Mum was a talented baker and she would produce shortbread, sponge cakes, Christmas cakes as well as dainty sandwiches and treats for visitors who were always welcomed.

One visitor we all looked forward to was Uncle George. While studying at Newbattle Abbey College and Edinburgh University he found his way every Sunday to relax with us all and to enjoy our mother's culinary treats. Perhaps, Dad and he talked of literary matters but that would all have gone above my head. I suspect the talk was more about football and politics and maybe the latest news from Orkney. He took a lively interest in his three nieces and I think our polite Edinburgh accents amused him.

From the perspective of a little six-year-old, as I was in 1956, he was a tall, gangly, curly-haired man with a large chin and smiling blue eyes. I was fascinated by his long fingers which seemed so expressive as he told us 'yarns' about people and events. I believed implicitly in all the stories he told us and it was years later when I realised that George was a born teller of tales with a playful taste for exaggeration.

The Hollywood and Oscar-nominated actress, Greer Garson, had Orcadian parents. According to George, Greer's mother and his were friends. He told me he remembered vividly being in his pram, side by side with the infant Greer while the ladies gossiped. He and Greer spent some time whacking each other over the head with their respective rattles, to their mothers' horror once they realised what was happening. According to George, Miss Garson had a splendid head of curls which, her mother feared, might never recover from such savage assault. It might even prevent her from becoming a film star. All this, I took in with wide-eyed innocence, delighting in the thrill of early celebrity scandal. It was many years later that I discovered the actress would have been 17 when George was an infant and that she had never lived in Orkney. (Despite their age difference and location, they died within a week of each other in 1996.)

A lot has been written about George's beliefs and his conversion to Catholicism. None of this concerned my sister, Pam, and me. We were oblivious to his religious persuasion as he solemnly officiated over the marriages of our various dolls. How lucky we were to have such a wonderful uncle who was so willing to participate in our games.

At one time, George was in lodgings in a flat in Marchmont, just along from where I attended Brownie meetings. I thought nothing of bringing along a friend to visit George after a trying hour or so tying knots and making Brownie promises. How his heart must have sunk when he heard us asking the landlady if my uncle was in. He always seemed happy to see us and listened intently as we told him of the evening's excitement. Best of all were the stories he told us which caused great hilarity. It never occurred to me that we may have interrupted his evening for half an hour or so.

While on holiday in Orkney in 1958, we were having a little tour of the mainland. Dad was driving and George sat in the front with his brother while we sat in the back, transfixed by the stories he told us of the places and the people. We passed the Brig o' Waithe, the place where the first civilian fatality of the Second World War took place as German planes jettisoned their remaining bombs on returning from their attack on Scapa Flow. In order that we did not dwell on this sad story, George pointed to a little stone cottage at the side of the road. 'You've no idea of the goings-on that took place over there,' he said. We were agog for some scandal. 'That wee house was once a den of iniquity, a drinking house a place where the men of Stromness walked to get away from their nagging wives and whining children. It was called The Golden Slipper and no decent man would be seen going near the place'. We thought this was thrilling and the story was embellished each time we passed the innocent cottage. By the end of our holiday, we knew the names of some of the scoundrels and misfits who frequented The Golden Slipper, those who'd been found in the ditch and those who'd lost all their money on a card game. Even we began to wonder when he told us the illuminated sign above the front door could be seen for miles.

He was adored by us all. As a child, I had no idea that he was a writer and was very excited when *Loaves and Fishes* was published in 1959. The TB he had suffered from as a very young man had left its mark and he was hospitalised in Edinburgh with severe bronchitis. I remember going with my mother to visit him. She warned me beforehand not to kiss him as he might be infectious. The fear of TB still lingered in the family throughout my childhood. His gaunt face was grey and his bony frame could be seen under his pyjamas. He struggled to speak without wheezing and coughing and there was a sputum cup on the bedside table. I remember feeling guilty at the relief I felt when visiting hour was over.

He recovered from this and other lung infections and we were delighted when he went to Moray House to train as a teacher. Unlike our father and their sister, Ruby, teaching was not to be his calling. I had no idea how much he hated it. I just enjoyed his tales of naughty pupils and how they ran wild when the real teacher left the room.

As I became a teenager, I developed a crush on the Beatles, but my parents were somewhat disapproving. How wonderful, then, to have an uncle who showed an interest in them, however feigned, and even took my side when begging to be allowed to stay up late to watch them on television. Every Sunday, he would turn up with newspaper clippings about them and I would stick them in my Beatles scrapbook.

My father had to retire early from teaching because of a heart problem. His sudden death at the age of 44 rocked our family. Granny Brown was staying with us for her annual holiday in Edinburgh and she was distraught. I was alarmed to see my beautiful, happy granny so stricken. We were all in shock and when George turned up later that day in a state of acute distress, I was further alarmed to see him sobbing. At 14, I had never seen a man cry before and it was a sight I shall never forget. How our brave, heartbroken mum coped with all this grief, I will never know.

Of course, I continued to have a relationship with George as we grew older. I had many holidays in Orkney, often staying with my granny and Uncle George and he continued to visit us in Edinburgh whenever he came south. My husband and three sons all loved George for his gentle sense of humour and, as he became more acclaimed in the literary world, his complete lack of self-importance.

I still wish I could have had apeep inside TheGolden Slipper!

'The Faithful Fishermen Still Sailed in Their Frail Boats Along the Atlantic Fringes'[1]

Liz Treacher

If authors could be summed up from just one sentence of their work then I believe that this line, from *For the Islands I Sing* by George Mackay Brown, might be up for consideration. It is as if he has condensed the essence of all his ideas and poured it into a little bottle. When the bottle stopper is taken off, the line escapes and, like a genie, Mackay Brown floats before us.

As a writer the line gives me permission to make every word count. It blurs the boundaries of poetry and prose, reminding me that the simplest thought can be imparted in an unforgettable way. As a reader the words offer a landscape and soundscape that propel me back to the North Sea of my childhood.

The line comes from near the beginning of Mackay Brown's autobiography, a point in the book when he is introducing us to the Orkney Islands, and it brings them immediately to life. We can see the islands scattered like gems and we can sense the continental shelf plunging suddenly into the deeper ocean. The alliteration of 'faithful fishermen', 'frail' and 'fringes' juxtaposes the fragility of men against the might of the sea. The soft sound of 'fringes' and the harsh vowels of 'Atlantic' further emphasise the difference in strength between water and man, while 'fringes' also beautifully describes the lacy coastline, dangling vulnerably into the ocean. If you say the

---

1 George Mackay Brown, *For the Islands I Sing* (2008), p.8.

words out loud, the fishermen seem to weave in and out of the water, like fine strands of wool weaving through a tapestry.

As I read the sentence, I am struck by the rhythm of the words. Not too short, not too long, a satisfying mouthful that teases the tongue but feels just right. The line settles into my mind, like a needle on the groove of a record.

Then there are the poetic ideas that the sentence evokes. The faithfulness of men going to sea every day, navigating all its moods 'in their frail boats'. There is a 5,000-year history humming in the words, a legend. Mackay Brown has written a single-lined hymn of respect for those that work on the sea, celebrating fishermen who are loyal not only to their jobs and their families, but also to the sea itself. 'Still sailed' means despite every shipwreck, every drowning. 'Still sailed' conjures up the vulnerability and tenacity not solely of those that fish, but all those who choose island life. The line reveals both our momentary lives and the permanence of island communities. It is a talisman that promises survival, a continuation of a heritage.

POSTSCRIPT

Leaving Harbour

In memory of George Mackay Brown

_____

Andrew Greig

April 1996: brisk day
waves flecked to the horizon
so bright so bright
His last murmur
in the Balfour Hospital, Kirkwall
I see hundreds of ships leaving harbour

Trust a poet
to hoard a good last line
then toss it overboard

marker buoy
as the faithful bilge pump
slows sputters stops

Yet he willed
a craft so well made
he could sink on an even keel

while all around
the shining waters poured in
through Orkney's harbouring arms

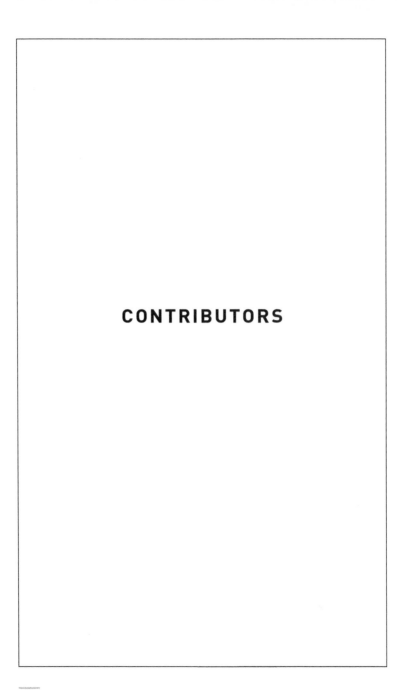

CONTRIBUTORS

ABOUT THE CONTRIBUTORS

Morag Anderson is an emerging Scottish poet based in Highland Perthshire. Her debut chapbook, *Sin Is Due to Open in a Room Above Kitty's* (2021), published by Fly on the Wall Press, explores human connection: concealed violence, love and everything in between. Her poetry appears in *Finished Creatures*, *Popshot Quarterly*, *Skylight 47*, *The Broken Spine Arts Collective* and *The Scotsman*, as well as in several anthologies. She was placed in The Blue Nib Chapbook VI Contest, shortlisted for the Bridport Poetry Prize and won Over the Edge New Poet.

Aileen Ballantyne is a national newspaper journalist turned poet. Her investigative journalism for *The Guardian* has twice been commended in the British Press Awards. Her poetry has won a series of recent major awards, including the Mslexia Poetry Prize, Poetry on the Lake at Orta san Giulio, the Scots prize at the Wigtown Poetry Festival, and a Scottish Book Trust New Writers Award. Her first poetry collection, *Taking Flight* (2019), explores flight in all its aspects, and commemorates the Lockerbie disaster in the voices of Lockerbie residents. She has a PhD in Creative Writing and Modern Poetry from the University of Edinburgh.

Gabrielle Barnby lives in Orkney and writes short stories, poetry and full-length fiction. Her work has been included in numerous anthologies and magazines and she is twice winner of the George Mackay Brown Fellowship Writing Competition. She has run creative writing workshops for many years, encouraging new writers and supporting creative discovery.

She is Programme Leader for Wirdsmit, Orkney's writing group for young people, and has a particular interest in writing for well-being. For more information about her work please visit gabriellebarnby.com.

Originally from Glasgow, **Pamela Beasant** has been living in Stromness, Orkney, for many years. She is a widely published poet and non-fiction writer, was the first George Mackay Brown Fellow in 2007, and has had seven plays commissioned and performed in Orkney. She directed the Orkney Writers' Course for the St Magnus International Festival from 2011-2017. She has given readings and led workshops all over the UK and in Brittany, Bratislava, Canada and Australia.

Linden Bicket is Lecturer in Literature and Religion in the School of Divinity at the University of Edinburgh. She is the author of *George Mackay Brown and the Scottish Catholic Imagination* (2017) and (with Professor Douglas Gifford) co-editor of *The Fiction of Robin Jenkins: Some Kind of Grace* (2017). Most recently she was editor (with Kirsteen McCue) of a new centenary edition of George Mackay Brown's *An Orkney Tapestry* (2021). Her research focuses on patterns of faith and scepticism in twentieth-century fiction and poetry.

Norman Bissell is the author of the poetry collection *Slate, Sea and Sky, A Journey from Glasgow to the Isle of Luing* (2015) (with photographs by Oscar Marzaroli), and the novel *Barnhill* (2019) about George Orwell's last years, both published by Luath Press. He is the Director of the Scottish Centre for Geopoetics and has co-edited nine issues of its journal *Stravaig*. An experienced teacher, he lives on the Isle of Luing in Argyll and is writing a memoir about his involvement in geopoetics over many years.

Edinburgh poet, **David Bleiman**, took to writing after a career as a trade union official. He won the Sangschaw prize 2020 for 'The Trebbler's Tale', written in a part-excavated and largely imagined dialect of Scots-Yiddish. In the same year he was shortlisted for the Wigtown Poetry and Pamphlet prizes. A first pamphlet, *This Kilt of Many Colours*, was published by Dempsey & Windle in March 2021. A celebration of the complexity of identity, it takes a sweeping historical view from the perspective of his own heritage and is written in a multilingual mixter-maxter including English, Scots, Yiddish and Spanish.

Helen Boden is a writer, educator and editor, based on the edge of Edinburgh. Widely published in poetry magazines and anthologies, her first collection *A Landscape to Figure In* will be published by Red Squirrel Press in 2021. She also collaborates with visual artists to make place-specific text, and responsive poems which have appeared in artists' books and pamphlets. A former lecturer in English and Scottish Literature at Edinburgh University, she has been an independent Literature professional since 2003, working across a broad range of community, healthcare, cultural and environmental settings, with a particular interests in Writing for Wellbeing and Writing and Place.

Colin Bramwell is a poet and performer from the Black Isle. He was the runner up for the 2020 Edwin Morgan Poetry Award. His work has appeared in *Gutter*, *The Scotsman* and *Northwords Now*. A pamphlet, *The Highland Citizenship Test* (2021), was recently published by Stewed Rhubarb. He is currently working towards a doctorate about Scots, translation and poetry, at St Andrews.

Niall Campbell is a poet originally from the Outer Hebrides of Scotland. He has two collections published by Bloodaxe Books: *Moontide* (2014) won the inaugural Edwin Morgan Poetry Award and the Saltire First Book of the Year; *Nocutary* (2019) was shortlisted for the Forward Prize for Best Collection.

A C Clarke has published five full poetry collections and six pamphlets, two of the latter, *Owersettin* (2016) and *Drochaid* (2019), in collaboration with Maggie Rabatski and Sheila Templeton. Her fifth full collection, *A Troubling Woman*, came out in 2017. She was one of four winners in the Cinnamon Press 2017 pamphlet competition with *War Baby*. She is currently working on an extensive series of poems about Gala Éluard, later Gala Dalí, and the Surrealist circles in which she moved. The first set of these, *Wedding Grief*, was published as a pamphlet by Tapsalteerie in 2021.

Stewart Conn lives in Edinburgh and was from 2002 to 2005 the city's inaugural Makar. Among his publications are *The Touch of Time: New & Selected Poems* (2014) and most recently *Aspects of Edinburgh*, with drawings by John Knight (2019). *Distances* (2000) contains a short memoir, 'Music and Muse: George Mackay Brown'. He directed *A Spell for Green Corn* and *The Voyage of Saint Brandon*, and himself dramatised *Beside the Ocean of Time* and *Greenvoe*, for BBC Radio. He is a patron of the George Mackay Brown Fellowship.

Erin Farley is a local historian, library worker and storyteller based in Dundee, working on projects around creative histories, place and traditions. She helps to run the Orkney Storytelling Festival and is happiest when a trip north is in the diary. In her spare time, she can usually be found swimming in the Tay.

Laura T Fyfe suffers from a chronic low boredom threshold. She writes poetry out of necessity, teaches out of compulsion and writes stories for fun. She facilitates writing communities across Scotland. Her work has been published in *Butcher's Dog*, *Postbox* and *Northwords Now*. She lives in river deep, mountain high Stirlingshire – and is the Stirling Makar.

Magi Gibson has seven poetry collections, the latest *I Like Your Hat* from Luath in 2020. She has won several writing awards, and has held Writing Fellowships with the Scottish Arts Council and the Royal Literary Fund. She has been Writer in Residence at GoMA in Glasgow and with Glasgow Women's Library. Her poetry is published in many literary magazines and in major anthologies including *Scottish Love Poems* (2002) and *Modern Scottish Women Poets* (2003) both published by Canongate, and *The Twentieth Century Book of Scottish Poetry* (2005) She has edited several magazines including *Pushing Out The Boat* and *The Poets' Republic*, and she runs Wild Women Writing.

Aberdeen based **Jo Gilbert** is a writer and spoken word artist. She writes in her native tongue of Doric and in English. A winner of multiple poetry slams, she has had work commissioned for festivals, art installations and films. Her most recent award is an Aberdeen Art Gallery and Museums micro commission to write poems in response to the art that will become part of the permanent collection.

John Glenday is the author of four collections of poetry, the most recent of which, *The Golden Mean*, won the 2015 Roehampton Poetry Prize. His work has appeared in newspapers and journals including the *London Review of Books*, *Poetry* (Chicago), *The Scotsman*, *The Guardian* and *Magma*, as well as in several anthologies. His *Selected Poems* was published by Picador Poetry in 2020 and a pamphlet, *The Firth*, by Mariscat Press in the same year.

Yvonne Gray is a writer and musician whose work has been published in magazines and anthologies in Scotland, Slovakia, Australia and the US. Her other publications include *Swappan the Mallimacks* (2006), *In the Hanging Valley* (2008) and *Hours* (2011). *Reflections* (2012), a collaboration with artist John Cumming, was commissioned by Woodend Barn, Banchory, and shortlisted for the Callum MacDonald Memorial Award in 2013. Currently, she is co-writing an opera libretto with playwright Rachel Lampert and composer Sally Lamb McCune for Opera Ithaca.

Andrew Greig is the author of 22 books of poetry, non-fiction and novels, the latest being respectively, *Later That Day* (2020), *You Know What You Could Be* (with Mike Heron, 2018) and *Rose Nicolson* (2021). He used to climb in the Himalayas and play golf in Scotland, now he plays banjo. A full-time writer for many years, he lives in Edinburgh and Orkney with his wife, novelist Lesley Glaister.

George Gunn is from Thurso in Caithness. In 2021, he will publish his 10th book of poems, *Chronicles of the First Light* (Drunk Muse Press). He has had over 50 plays produced for stage and radio, the latest being 'Call Me Mister Bullfinch' (The Royal Lyceum Theatre commission) and 'The Fallen Angels of the Moine' (Dogstar Theatre, proposed tour 2022). He writes for the magazine *Bella Caledonia* and is currently the Caithness Makar with Lyth Arts Centre. He has been described by *Scotland on Sunday* as 'a poet of energy and lyricism. Fearless'.

A keen sailor, **Mandy Haggith** lives in Assynt, Scotland, and teaches Literature and Creative Writing at the University of the Highlands and Islands. She has four published poetry collections, a tree poetry anthology, a non-fiction book about paper and five novels including an Iron Age historical trilogy, *The Stone Stories* (2018-20).

Nat Hall is a Norman-born, Shetland-based poet and visual artist, educated on French and British shores in Aix-en-Provence, Oxford and Edinburgh. She is a member of Shetland Arts, the Scottish Centre for Geopoetics and the Federation of Writers (Scotland); and a contributor to the *New Shetlander*, *Northwords Now*, *Stravaig*, *The Poetry Scotland's Open Mouse*, *Artipeeps* (England) and *Poemata* (Canada). Her work has been anthologised in Shetland, Scotland, England and Canada. She is co-author of *From Shore to Shoormal/D'un rivage à l'autre* (2012), author of *Compass Head* (2016) and translator of Georges Dif, *Shetland* (2018). She is working on her second poetry collection.

Simon W Hall is the author of *The History of Orkney Literature* (John Donald, 2010), the first full survey of the literature of the Orkney Islands. It was a joint winner of the Saltire Society's First Book of the Year award (2010) and has been translated into Japanese. He has made Orkney language translations of Julia Donaldson's popular books for children, *The Gruffalo* and *The Gruffalo's Child*, published as *The Orkney Gruffalo* (2015) and *The Gruffalo's Bairn* (2016). Simon is a head teacher in Orkney, and he blogs at brisknortherly.

Jenifer Harley, originally from East Lothian, now lives in Livingston with her husband Dave. Retired from the civil service a few years ago, she was chair of the Federation of Writers (Scotland) from 2018 to June 2021 and is an active member of West Lothian Writers. She writes mainly for pleasure but does enjoy attending and performing at spoken word events. Her short stories and poems have been published in several anthologies and chapbooks.

Anne Hay comes from Perth and lives in Edinburgh. Her writing career started with comedy and short fiction broadcast on BBC Radio 4 and Radio Scotland. She has had poems published in literary magazines including *Gutter*, *Magma*, *Envoi* and *Northwords Now*. Her first pamphlet will be published by Red Squirrel Press in 2023.

W N Herbert was born in Dundee and lives in a lighthouse in North Shields. He is mostly published by Bloodaxe Books, who brought out his latest collection, *The Wreck of the Fathership*, in 2020. He teaches poetry at Newcastle University, and was until recently Dundee's first Makar, or city laureate. In his head he still is.

Andy Jackson has published three collections of poetry, including most recently *The Saints Are Coming* (Blue Diode Press, 2020). He has edited nine anthologies including *Split Screen* (2012) and *Double Bill* (2013), both published by Red Squirrel; *Whaleback City* (2013) with W N Herbert; and *Scotia Extremis* (2019) with Brian Johnstone. He was Makar of the Federation of Writers (Scotland) in 2017 and is currently the co-editor of the long-running broadsheet *Poetry Scotland*.

Caroline Johnstone works part time as a senior legal employment advisor and in running wellbeing workshops. She is also an author and poet. Originally from Northern Ireland, she now lives on the coast in Ayrshire. Her poems have been published widely in the UK, Ireland, US and Australia. In 2019, she won the Waterways Storymaking Festival Award, the Imprint Writing Award and the Beyond Borders Round III competition and was longlisted for the Over The Edge New Writer of the Year.

Asif Khan is the director of the Scottish Poetry Library, which houses the nation's collection of modern Scottish poetry. As well as a career in public library engagement, he has worked across arts and heritage, including the role of senior policy advisor at the Museums Libraries & Archives Council. He has strong international connections from his time as an associate with Arts Council England's Cultural Leadership Programme, for which he wrote the visual art strategy for Barbados. He has also worked in partnership with the Jamaican Government in support of their poet laureate initiative. He sits on the Advisory Committee for British Council (Scotland) and is a board member of Culture Perth & Kinross and the Robert Burns Ellisland Trust.

Ingrid Leonard comes from Orkney, which inspires much of her work. She has an MA in 'Writing Poetry' from Newcastle University and she is currently a PhD student at the University of Aberdeen, focusing on writing poetry in Orcadian Scots. Her work has appeared in *Pushing Out The Boat*, *New Writing Scotland*, *Northwords Now*, *Brittle Star* and *The Interpreter's House*. She lives in Orkney and Vilnius.

Marjorie Lotfi's writing is about belonging and finding a home in the places in between. Her poems have won competitions, been published widely in the UK and abroad and performed on BBC Radio 4. *Refuge*, poems about her childhood in revolutionary Iran, was published by Tapsalteerie Press in 2018. She was an Ignite Fellow with the Scottish Book Trust and writes as part of the 12 Collective.

Christine De Luca writes in English and Shetlandic, her mother tongue. She was appointed Edinburgh's Makar for 2014-2017. She has had seven poetry collections published and five bi-lingual volumes (French, Italian, Icelandic, Norwegian and English). She enjoys collaborating with musicians and artists. She has also written and translated stories for children and recently completed a second novel. She has judged several poetry competitions, most recently for Wigtown Book Festival in 2019. She is a member of Edinburgh's long-standing poetry platform Shore Poets.

Marcas Mac an Tuairneir/Mark Spencer Turner writes in Gaelic, English and Polari and has been shortlisted for the Wigtown Scottish Gaelic Poetry Prize four times in six years, winning in 2017. He has published two collections and a co-authored pamphlet. His third collection, *Dùileach: Elemental*, was published by Evertype in 2021. A fourth, *Polaris*, is expected by the end of 2021. He is one of Gaeldom's most dynamic singer-songwriters and his single 'Nochd' was released in May 2021.

Pàdraig MacAoidh/Peter Mackay is a poet, broadcaster and lecturer. He works in the School of English at the University of St Andrews. His most recent books are *Nàdur De/Some Kind of* (2020), *100 Dàn as Fheàrr Leinn/100 Favourite Gaelic Poems*, with Jo MacDonald (2020) and *This Strange Loneliness: Heaney's Wordsworth* (2021).

Stuart MacBeath is from John o' Groats. He completed postgraduate research on George Mackay Brown at Glasgow University, focusing on Mackay Brown's early journalism for the *Orkney Herald*. He has produced educational materials on Scottish writers such as George Mackay Brown, Iain Crichton Smith and Sorley MacLean for the BBC. He is a principal teacher in secondary education.

Hamish MacDonald's poetry has been published by Clydeside Press, Itchy Coo and in magazines and anthologies. Recent works include *Wilson's Ornithology & Burds in Scots* (Scotland Street Press, 2020) and *Kilbowie Dreams* (2020). His plays include *Factor 9* (Dogstar Theatre), an uncompromising exposé of the NHS contaminated blood scandal. He is author of the novel *The Gravy Star* (2001). He was Robert Burns Writing Fellow for Dumfries and Galloway Arts Association 2003-6 and Scots Scriever at the National Library of Scotland 2015-17. As the Bankies Bard, he is Poet in Residence for Clydebank FC.

Fiona MacInnes is from Stromness where she has lived most of her life. She trained as a painter at Edinburgh College of Art. Her first collection of poetry, 'To Step Among Wrack', was published in 1988 with an introduction by George Mackay Brown. Her poetry and short stories have been published in various collections including *Shorts, The Macallan Scotland on Sunday Short Story Collection* (1998). In 2013, her novel, *Iss*, was published and described by George Gunn as, 'the most important novel to come out of Orkney since George Mackay Brown died'. She is currently reviewing a second novel in draft.

Ross MacKay was the recipient of the William Soutar Writing Prize 2020 for his poem 'We Called Him Noah' and a Tom McGrath Trust Maverick Award. Ross previously worked in theatre as the artistic director of Tortoise in a Nutshell, Edinburgh based virtual theatre company. His productions toured all over the world, and received prestigious awards including a Scotsman Fringe First and a Critic's Pick from *The New York Times*.

Rob A Mackenzie is a Glaswegian poet, editor and reviewer. He lives in Leith. His poetry collections are *The Opposite of Cabbage* (2009), *The Good News* (2013) and *The Book of Revelation* (2020), all published by Salt. He is reviews editor for *Magma Poetry* magazine and runs Blue Diode Press.

Jim Mackintosh is the Makar of both the Federation of Writers (Scotland) and the Cateran EcoMuseum. He is the Poet in Chief at the Hampden Collection and poetry editor of *Nutmeg Magazine*, the only sports journal in the UK with a poetry section. He is the Programme Manager for the Hamish Matters Festival and, between 2016 and 2019, he was the Poet in Residence at St Johnstone FC. He is the author of six collections of poetry, the latest being *Flipstones* published by Tippermuir Books in 2018 and also editor of two other anthologies, *Mind The Time* (2017) for Football Memories and *The Darg* (2019) celebrating the centenary of Hamish Henderson's birth.

Paul Malgrati is a poet and academic from France, residing in Scotland since 2016. His work, inspired by French symbolism and Scottish modernism, is a poetic exploration of the 'Auld Alliance', blending Franco-Scots languages and traditions. His debut collection, *Poèmes Ecossais*, shortlisted for the Edwin Morgan Poetry Award in 2020, is forthcoming with Blue Diode

Press (2022). In 2020, he completed a PhD at the University of St Andrews, focussing on the political legacy of Robert Burns. He now works as a research assistant in Scottish literature at the University of Glasgow.

Marion McCready lives in Dunoon, Argyll. Her poems have been published widely including in *Poetry*, *Edinburgh Review* and the *Glasgow Herald*. She won a Scottish Book Trust New Writers Award in 2013 and the Melita Hume Poetry Prize for her first full-length collection *Tree Language* published by Eyewear Publishing in 2014. Her second collection *Madame Ecosse* was published in 2017 also by Eyewear Publishing.

Cáit O'Neill McCullagh is a straying archaeologist. She has co-produced exhibitions, films and new writing with people throughout the Highlands and Islands, and curated in museums in Ross, Lismore and Inverness. Now in the final year of a PhD with Heriot-Watt University, she writes at home in Easter Ross about researching with people across Orkney and Shetland who transform their maritime heritages into creative ethnologies for resourcing their island futures. Cáit's writing has recently turned to poetry. She was a joint winner of the *Boyne Writers Festival* Poetry Day Competition 2021, and her poems have been published in *Northwords Now*, *Bella Caledonia* and the *Banyan Review*.

Beth McDonough's poetry is published in *Magma*, *Gutter* and elsewhere. She was Writer in Residence at Dundee Contemporary Arts (2014-16), and an art teacher for many years before that. Her first solo pamphlet, *Lamping for Pickled Fish* (2019), is published by 4Word and her site-specific poem will be installed soon on the Corbenic Poetry Path. She may be found swimming year round in the Tay, beachcombing and foraging nearby.

Jane McKie has a few books and pamphlets, some resulting from collaborations with artists. *Morocco Rococo*, from Cinnamon Press, won the Sundial/SAC award for best first book of 2007. Her most recent collection is *Quiet Woman, Stay* (2020). She is a member of the Edinburgh-based Shore Poets, and writes with the poetry collective 12. She has loved the work of George Mackay Brown for decades.

Hugh McMillan lives in south west Scotland. His poetry is published widely. His new collections, *Haphazardly in the Starless Night* and *Whit If? Poems aboot Scottish History* are due in Autumn 2021 from Luath. He has won numerous prizes and competitions including the Smith/Doorstep Pamphlet Prize, the Cardiff International Poetry Competition and the Callum MacDonald Prize. He has been shortlisted for many more.

Julie McNeill works with children with special educational needs. She writes poetry and short fiction and is the Makar of the SWNT Poets Society and Bairns Bard at the Hampden Collection. Her first book for children, *Mission Dyslexia*, launched in March 2021 published by JKP Books.

Victoria McNulty is a performance poet, writer and community practitioner from Glasgow. Her writing has been published by Speculative Books, while her contributions have been circulated in anthologies and periodicals including releases by *Nutmeg*, the Joe Strummer Foundation and Neu Reekie! Her performances have gathered critical acclaim, being programmed at events across the UK and Ireland including, the Edinburgh Book Festival, Féile and Phobail (West Belfast Festival), BBC 6 Festival and the James Connolly Festival (Dublin). In 2017, she toured her show Confessionals (Sonnet Youth) nationally and is currently producing her latest work Exiles, directed by Kevin P Gilday and David Hayman Jr (Fair Pley).

Born and raised in Orkney, **Alison Miller** is a freelance author, editor and creative writing tutor. Her first novel, *Demo* (Penguin, 2006), was shortlisted for the Saltire First Book of the Year Award. Since her return to Orkney, she has had poems, stories and essays anthologised in a variety of publications. As part of the George Mackay Brown Fellowship, she has been involved in organising events for his centenary in 2021. She also works with Orkney Voices and is currently editing a collection of their writing in Orcadian to be published in 2021.

Alexander Moffat RSA is an artist and teacher. In 1979, he joined the staff of the Glasgow School of Art where he was Head of Painting from 1992 until his retirement in 2005. His portraits of the major poets of the Scottish Renaissance movement now hang in the Scottish National Portrait Gallery and his paintings are represented in many public and private collections including the Yale Centre for British Art, USA and the Pushkin Museum in Moscow.

Andrew Motion is an acclaimed poet and writer. He read English at University College, Oxford, and subsequently spent two years writing about the poetry of Edward Thomas for an MLitt. From 1976 to 1980, he taught English at the University of Hull, from 1980 to 1972, he edited the *Poetry Review* and from 1982 to 1989, he was Editorial Director and Poetry Editor at Chatto & Windus. He is a Fellow of the Royal Society of Literature and a patron of the George Mackay Brown Fellowship. Between 1999 and 2009, he was the Poet Laureate during which time he founded the Poetry Archive and wrote poetry engaged with both contemporary events and everyday life. He has published widely and won numerous awards for his poetry and prose. In 2009, he was conferred as Knight Bachelor.

Duncan Stewart Muir grew up on the island of Islay. He now lives in Glasgow where he teaches English. His poetry has been published in *The Poetry Review*, *PN Review*, *Gutter* and *New Writing Scotland*. In 2018, he received a New Writer's Award from The Scottish Book Trust.

Donald S Murray is a Gaelic speaking poet, author and occasional dramatist who was raised in Ness, Lewis, and now lives in Shetland. His novel, *As the Women Lay Dreaming* (2018), about the Iolaire disaster of 1 January 1919 won the Paul Torday Memorial Prize for 2020. His novel, *In a Veil of Mist*, was published in March 2021 and was chosen as The Times Historical Book of the Month. His non-fiction book, *For the Safety of All – the Story of Scotland's Lighthouses*, appears in July 2021.

Hamish Napier is a folk musician and composer. He is a multiple Scots Trad Music Awards winner and nominee, winning *Session Musician of the Year* and *Album of the Year* (for *The Woods*), with nominations in over a dozen other categories. He has performed or recorded with leading Scottish artists including Eddi Reader, Julie Fowlis (*Brave*), Duncan Chisholm (*Wolfstone*), Blue Rose Code, Ross Ainslie, Jarlath Henderson and *Capercaillie* founding members Charlie McKerron, Donald Shaw and Karen Matheson. His *Strathspey Pentaology* is an ambitious project to create five albums of original compositions dedicated to his homeland. The first three albums, *The River* (2016), *The Railway* (2018) and *The Woods* (2020) have received 5-star reviews in the national press and work has already begun on the last two: *The Hill* (2022) and *The Sky* (2024).

Màiri Anna NicUalraig/Mary Ann Kennedy is a Glasgow-born Gael, brought up in the multicultural southside. She is a 2020 New Writer awardee with the Scottish Books Trust/Comhairle nan Leabhraichean, and 2019 Gaelic Singer of the Year at the Scots Trad Music Awards. Music and song are her earliest memories, as part of a well-known tradition-bearer family. She trained as a classical musician at the RSAMD in Glasgow and RNCM in Manchester. She joined the BBC in 1993, before returning to a freelance life combining music and broadcasting. She is co-director of the residential studio and creative hub Watercolour Music in Lochaber.

Stuart A Paterson is a native Scots speaker, writer and activist originally from Ayrshire who now lives in Galloway. From 2017-18 he was the official BBC Scotland Poet in Residence and from 2015-16 was Poet in Residence with the Scots Language Centre. In 2019, the UNESCO Year of Indigenous Minority Languages, Stuart was Visiting Lecturer in Language at Rhodes University, South Africa, and led Scots Master-classes at Northern Ireland's Ulster Scots Language Week in Belfast. Author of several collections and widely published, anthologised and filmed worldwide, he received an Eric Gregory Award from the UK Society of Authors in 1992 and a Robert Louis Stevenson Fellowship from the Scottish Book Trust in 2014. He was voted Scots Writer o the Year at the 2020 national Scots Language Awards.

Nalini Paul's poetry is inspired by landscapes, memory and subjectivity. Her first collection, *Skirlags* (2009), was short-listed for the Callum Macdonald Memorial Award in 2010 and her recent collection, The Raven's Song (2015) is inspired by raven and crow myths from Orkney, Shetland and Canada. She has collaborated with visual artists, dancers, musicians, archaeologists and the RSPB. Nalini was George Mackay Brown Writing Fellow in Orkney (2009-10); Robert Louis

Stevenson Fellow in Grez-sur-Loing, France (Scottish Book Trust, 2017); and took part in the 'New Passages' residency in Stornoway and Kolkata, India (Edinburgh International Book Festival, 2017, 2018). She has a PhD in postcolonial studies and works as a lecturer for The Glasgow School of Art.

Louise Peterkin is a poet and editor from Edinburgh. She is a recipient of a New Writers Award from the Scottish Book Trust. Her poems have appeared in publications including *The Dark Horse*, *Magma* and *The North*. In 2020, she was longlisted for the National Poetry Competition. She is assistant poetry editor for *The Interpreter's House* and is co-editor, along with Rob A Mackenzie, of *Spark: Poetry and Art Inspired by the Novels of Muriel Spark* (2016). Her first poetry collection, *The Night Jar*, was published by Salt in 2020.

Paul S Philippou is Honorary Research Fellow in History at the University of Dundee, a member of the Centre for Scottish Culture and joint editor/coordinator of The Soutar Project (the publication of the complete poetry and prose of William Soutar). He is the author of seven books which cover a range of historical and literary themes from Walter Scott to the Spanish Civil War. He is a regular contributor to the *Journal of Scottish Labour History* wherein he draws upon his PhD thesis (University of Dundee) on the labour and trade union movement in Scotland, c1867-c1922.

Sheenagh Pugh lived for many years in Wales but now lives in Shetland. She has published many poetry collections with Seren, also two novels and a critical study on fan fiction. Her novel *Kirstie's Witnesses* (1998) was reprinted in 2021.

John Quinn is an ex-teacher, writer and performer from Dundee. His poetry in Scots and English has appeared in publications including *Northwords Now*, *Poetry Scotland*, *Lallans* and *The Darg*. He is the author of a historical novel, *The Eyes of Grace O'Malley* (2018), and a play, *O Halflins an Hecklers an Weavers an Weemin*, about Dundee and jute. An album of songs for which he wrote lyrics, 'More Than Seven Wonders', is due for release in 2021 as a fundraiser for a Tayside children's charity.

A former English teacher turned freelance science writer, **Larissa Reid** lives on Scotland's east coast where she balances her writing life with bringing up her daughters. She writes poetry and prose, with notable publications in *Northwords Now*, *Reliquiae* and *The Darg*, and has had a poem shortlisted for the 2020 Janet Coats Memorial Prize. She's intrigued by visible and invisible boundary lines in landscapes – geological faultlines, myth and reality, and edge-lines of land and sea. She is also a founder member of the Edinburgh-based writing collective Twisted::Colon.

Orcadian poet **Olive M Ritch**, who now lives and works in Aberdeen, was the recipient of the Scottish Book Trust's Next Chapter Award 2020. She has been published in many literary magazines, anthologies and websites including *Poetry Review*, *Agenda*, *Gutter*, *The Guardian*, *New Writing Scotland*, *The Poetry Cure* (2005), *Don't Bring Me No Rocking Chair* (2013), *In Protest: 150 Poems for Human Rights* (2013) and the Scottish Poetry Library. Her work has also been broadcast on Radio 4.

James Robertson is a poet, short story writer and novelist. He is also a co-founder of and contributing editor to Itchy Coo, which specialises in publishing books in Scots for young readers. He has published seven novels, including *Joseph*

Knight (2003), *The Testament of Gideon Mack* (2006), *And the Land Lay Still* (2010) and, most recently, *News of the Dead* (2021). He stays in Angus.

Gail Ross was the MSP for Caithness, Sutherland and Ross from 2016-2021. Before that, she was a Highland councillor for Wick and civic leader of Caithness. She lives in Wick with her husband, Stewart and 11-year-old son, Max. She's a keen gardener and likes to spend time by the sea, walking Monty the dog and writing. She is Scotland Patron of Dignity in Dying, Patron of the Caithness Broch Project and a member of the Mey Games Committee. She has been writing on and off since sixth year in high school and takes her inspiration from people she meets or places she's been, often with a leaning towards the melancholy side of life.

Finola Scott writes in Scots and English. Her poems are on posters, tapestries, postcards and published widely including in *New Writing Scotland*, *The High Window*, *PB* and *Lighthouse*. Her work was commissioned by StAnza International Poetry Festival for inclusion in a multi-media installation. She focuses on little things. With her grandchildren she writes poems and feeds birds. Her pamphlet *Much left unsaid* was published by Red Squirrel Press in 2019.

Leela Soma was born in Madras, India, and now lives in Glasgow. Her poems and short stories have been published in several anthologies, and publications. She has published three novels, short stories and two collections of poetry; and a chapbook, 'Chintz', published by Dreich Press. Her poems have been published in *Gutter*, *The Blue Nib*, *Anthropocene*, *Black Bough Poems*, *The Glasgow Review of Books* and many others. She was nominated for the Pushcart Prize 2020 and has been appointed Scriever 2021 for the Federation of Writers, Scotland. She has just been added to the Scottish Poetry Library's Guide to Scottish Poets. Some of her work reflects her dual Scotland-India heritage.

Ian Spring is a writer and publisher living in Perth. He has written extensively on Scottish cultural history and folk song, including two books on Glasgow. He also writes poetry and prose and his latest book of short fiction, *The Stone Mirror*, was published in April 2021.

Gerda Stevenson, writer, actor, director and singer-songwriter, works in theatre, opera, TV, radio and film. Her poetry, drama and prose are widely published, staged and broadcast. Her play, Federer Vs Murray, toured to New York in 2012. She was nominated as MG ALBA Scots Singer of the Year for her album 'Night Touches Day'. Her published poetry includes: Inside & Out – the Art of Christian Small (2019), Edinburgh (2019) with landscape photographer Allan Wright, If This Were Real (2013) and QUINES: Poems in Tribute to Women of Scotland ([2018], 2020), both also published in Italian translations by Edizioni Ensemble, Rome (2017 and 2021 respectively).

Courtney Stoddart is an acclaimed Scottish-Caribbean poet and performer, born and raised in Edinburgh. Her work focuses on racism, imperialism and challenging the corporate state. Having started performing in April 2019, she has performed at venues such as the Traverse Theatre, Scottish National Portrait Gallery and Leith Theatre. In June 2019, she took part in the BBC Radio 1xtra and BBC Contains Strong Language Festival Word's First Talent Scheme, making it to the final 12. As of 2021, she was announced as an Ignite Fellow with the Scottish Book Trust.

Kenny Taylor edits *Northwords Now* from his home on the Black Isle. Principally a writer of non-fiction drawn from environmental science, literature and history, he works in print and broadcast media and through talks and performances. His essays and poetry have appeared in several recent anthologies and his many books include the international-prize-shortlisted *Natural Heartlands*. He has returned to Orkney many times since the 1980s, including to stay on uninhabited islands, and has relished the work of George Mackay Brown throughout.

Ros Taylor lived her very early years in the parish of St Margaret's Hope in Orkney. Her father, the brother of George Mackay Brown, was a school teacher there until the family moved to Edinburgh where she remained until leaving to become a student teacher. After qualifying, she taught in various schools until finally settling in the Borders with her husband, Paul, and three young sons. She went on to specialise in deaf education and was a campaigner for British Sign Language to be used in mainstream schools. She has a lifelong interest in drama and helped found Tweed Theatre in Peebles.

Sheila Templeton writes in both Scots and English. She was nominated as Scots Writer of the Year in the 2020 Scots Language Awards and has also won a number of poetry prizes, the latest being the 2019 Neil Gunn Writing Competition (Poetry) and the 2020 James McCash Scots Language Poetry Prize. She is a previous Makar of the Federation of Writers (Scotland) and is getting through these strange times as best she can, with much joy in having become a granny in 2020. Her most recent poetry collection is *Clyack* (2021).

Samuel Tongue's first collection of poetry, *Sacrifice Zones*, was published by Red Squirrel in 2020. He has published two pamphlets: *Hauling-Out* (2016) and *Stitch* (2018). His poems have appeared in *Butcher's Dog*, *Magma*, *The Compass*, *Finished Creatures*, *Gutter*, *The Interpreter's House* and elsewhere.

Liz Treacher is an author and writing tutor based in Sutherland. She has written three novels published by Skelbo Press: *The Wrong Envelope* (2018), *The Wrong Direction* (2018) and *The Unravelling* (2020). She has an academic interest in language used during conflict and researched metaphor and metonymy in First World War letters for an MLitt. She also works as an art photographer, exploring light and how it transforms everyday life.

Lynn Valentine lives on the Black Isle with husband and dogs. She has a Scots language pamphlet out with Hedgehog Poetry (July 2021) and is working towards her debut poetry collection which will be published by Cinnamon Press early in 2022. She was one of five 'North' poets to be commissioned by the Scottish Poetry Library as part of their Champions 2020 project. She visited Orkney in 2019, fell in love with the place and took a wee pilgrimage in the footsteps of George Mackay Brown.

Stephen Watt is from Dumbarton and the author of five poetry collections. Since 2016, he has been the Poet in Residence at Dumbarton Football Club and has previously been the Makar for the Federation of Writers (Scotland) and inaugural Poet in Chief for The Hampden Collection. As well as winning the StAnza International Digital Poetry prize, among other notable awards, he has edited two punk poetry collections on behalf of the Joe Strummer Foundation (*Ashes To Activists*, 2018) and Buzzcocks (*Pogo Serotonin*, 2020).

Jay Whittaker lives and works in Edinburgh. She has published two poetry collections, both with Cinnamon Press: *Wristwatch*, which was Scottish Poetry Book of the Year (Saltire Society Literary Awards) 2018, and *Sweet Anaesthetist* (2020). She enjoys performing her poems, and has been well-received by audiences at the StAnza International Poetry Festival and other poetry and spoken word events in Scotland and beyond.

Christie Williamson comes fae Yell. His poyims have been widely published, and collected in *Oo an Feddirs* (2015) and *Doors tae Naewye* (2020). He lives in Glasgow. His translations of Federico Garcia Lorca's poetry into Shetland dialect was published in 2009 by Hansel Co-operative Press. It was a joint-winner of the Calum Macdonald Memorial Award 2010.

Neil Young hails from Belfast and, after many migrations, now lives in Aberdeenshire. He worked as a labourer, kitchen porter, barman and stage-hand before becoming a journalist, going on to report everywhere from New York post-9/11 to the Gaza Strip. Neil's publications include *Lagan Voices* (2011), *The Parting Glass – 14 Sonnets* (2016), *Jimmy Cagney's Long-Lost Kid Half-Brother* (2017), *Shrapnel* (2019) and *After the Riot* (2021). He is the publishing editor of *The Poets' Republic* magazine and Drunk Muse Press.

OTHER TITLES BY TIPPERMUIR BOOKS

PAST

Spanish Thermopylae (2009)

Battleground Perthshire (2009)

Perth: Street by Street (2012)

Born in Perthshire (2012)

In Spain with Orwell (2013)

Trust (2014)

Perth: As Others Saw Us (2014)

Love All (2015)

A Chocolate Soldier (2016)

The Early Photographers of Perthshire (2016)

Taking Detective Novels Seriously:
The Collected Crime Reviews of Dorothy L Sayers (2017)

Walking with Ghosts (2017)

No Fair City: Dark Tales from Perth's Past (2017)

The Tale o the Wee Mowdie that wantit tae ken wha
keeched on his heid (2017)

Hunters: Wee Stories from the Crescent:
A Reminiscence of Perth's Hunter Crescent (2017)

A Little Book of Carol's (2018)

Flipstones (2018)

Perth: Scott's Fair City: The Fair Maid of Perth &
Sir Walter Scott – A Celebration & Guided Tour (2018)

God, Hitler, and Lord Peter Wimsey: Selected Essays,
Speeches and Articles by Dorothy L Sayers (2019)

Perth & Kinross: A Pocket Miscellany:
A Companion for Visitors and Residents (2019)

The Piper of Tobruk: Pipe Major Robert Roy, MBE, DCM (2019)

The 'Gig Docter o Athole': Dr William Irvine & The Irvine
Memorial Hospital (2019)

Afore the Highlands: The Jacobites in Perth, 1715-16 (2019)

'Where Sky and Summit Meet': Flight Over Perthshire –
A History: Tales of Pilots, Airfields, Aeronautical Feats,
& War (2019)

Diverted Traffic (2020)

Authentic Democracy: An Ethical Justification of Anarchism
(2020)

'If Rivers Could Sing': A Scottish River Wildlife Journey.
A Year in the Life of the River Devon as it flows through the
Counties of Perthshire, Kinross-shire & Clackmannanshire
(2020)

A Squatter o Bairnrhymes (2020)

In a Sma Room Songbook: From the Poems by William Soutar
(2020)

The Nicht Afore Christmas: the much-loved yuletide tale in
Scots (2020)

2021

Ice Cold Blood (David Millar, 2021)

The Perth Riverside Nursery & Beyond: A Spirit of Enterprise
and Improvement (Elspeth Bruce and Pat Kerr, 2021)

Fatal Duty: The Scottish Police Force to 1952:
Cop Killers, Killer Cops & More (Gary Knight, 2021)

The Shanter Legacy: The Search for the Grey Mare's Tail
(Garry Stewart, 2021)

'Dying to Live': The Story of Grant McIntyre, Covid's Sickest
Patient (Grant and Amanda McIntyre, 2021)

FORTHCOMING

A Scottish Wildlife Odyssey (Keith Broomfield, 2021)

William Soutar: Collected Poetry, Volume I (Published Work)
(Kirsteen McCue and Paul S Philippou (editors), 2021)

William Soutar: Collected Poetry, Volume II (Unpublished Work) (Kirsteen McCue and Paul S Philippou (editors), 2022)

Perthshire 101 (Andy Jackson (editor), 2022)

'A War of Two Halves' and 'Sweet FA'
(Tim Barrow, Paul Beeson and Bruce Strachan, 2022)

Berries Fae Banes: An owersettin in Scots o the poems bi Pino Mereu scrievit in tribute tae Hamish Henderson
(Jim Mackintosh, 2022)

All Tippermuir Books titles are available from bookshops and online booksellers.

They can also be purchased directly (with free postage & packing (UK only) – minimum charges for overseas delivery) from www.tippermuirbooks.co.uk.

Tippermuir Books Ltd can be contacted at mail@tippermuirbooks.co.uk

TIPPERMUIR
· BOOKS LIMITED ·